ADA CARTIANU

THE

HUMAN

COMPASS

EXPLORING THE SPECTRUM OF HUMANITY

HUMANIST PHILOSOPHY AND EMOTIONAL INTELLIGENCE

THE HUMAN COMPASS
EXPLORING THE SPECTRUM OF HUMANITY
HUMANIST PHILOSOPHY AND EMOTIONAL INTELLIGENCE

TABLE OF CONTENTS

INTRODUCTION

Weaving Together Humanism, Emotion, and Understanding

The human story is an epic poem, an unfolding narrative etched across the vast canvas of existence. It is a story of triumphs and tragedies, of soaring aspirations and crushing disappointments, of the quiet whispers of joy and the thunderous pronouncements of despair. It is a story written in the language of emotion, a language both universal and deeply personal, a language that speaks to the very core of what it means to be human. Within this grand narrative, each individual life forms a unique verse, a distinct melody within the larger symphony of being. We are each a special link in this intricate tapestry, laced together by the shared experience of existence, yet distinct in our colors, textures, and patterns. This tapestry, rich in its complexity and breathtaking in its scope, is what we call the *Human Spectrum – a Human Compass.*

For millennia, philosophers and thinkers have grappled with the fundamental questions of human existence: What is the nature of consciousness? What drives our actions? What is the meaning of life? Traditional approaches have often sought to define humanity through a limited lens, focusing on rationality as the defining characteristic, often at the expense of the rich emotional landscape that colors our thoughts and actions. This emphasis on reason has created a false dichotomy, a separation between mind and body, between thought and feeling, that fails to capture the holistic nature of the human experience. We are not simply rational beings; we are emotional beings, driven by a complex interplay of feelings, desires, and motivations. To ignore this fundamental aspect of our being is to understand only half the story.

This book, *The Human Compass: A Path to Greater Understanding*, seeks to bridge this divide, to weave together the threads of reason and emotion, to explore the full breadth and depth of the human experience. It proposes a journey of discovery, a path towards a more nuanced and compassionate understanding of ourselves and others. Central to this journey are two powerful frameworks: humanistic philosophy and emotional intelligence.

Humanistic philosophy, with its emphasis on human potential, inherent goodness, and the search for meaning, provides a guiding light. It reminds us of the inherent dignity and worth of every individual, regardless of their background, beliefs, or circumstances. It champions the power of self-actualization, the drive towards personal growth and fulfillment that resides within each of us. It encourages us to embrace our individuality, to celebrate our differences, and to strive towards becoming the best versions of ourselves.

Emotional intelligence, on the other hand, provides a practical framework for understanding and navigating the complex world of emotions. It recognizes that emotions are not simply irrational impulses to be suppressed, but rather valuable sources of information, providing insights into our needs, our values, and our relationships. Emotional intelligence empowers us to develop self-awareness, to understand and manage our own emotions, to empathize with others, and to build strong and meaningful connections.

The Human Spectrum is not a static entity; it is a dynamic and ever-evolving landscape. It is shaped by a multitude of factors, including our individual experiences, our cultural backgrounds, our social contexts, and our biological predispositions. It is a spectrum that encompasses the full range of human emotions, from the heights of ecstasy to the depths of despair, and everything in between. It is a spectrum that reflects the diversity of human thought, behavior, and expression.

To truly understand the human condition, we must embrace the full spectrum of human experience. We must move beyond simplistic categorizations and recognize the inherent complexity and fluidity of human nature. We must cultivate empathy and compassion, recognizing that every individual's story is worthy of our attention and respect. This book is an invitation to embark on this journey of understanding, to explore the tapestry of being, and to discover the rich and multifaceted nature of the *Human Spectrum*. It is a journey that promises not only greater self-awareness but also a deeper appreciation for the shared humanity that connects us all.

The evolution of humanity is not just a story of technological advancement, but a journey towards greater emotional awareness. It is in cultivating emotional intelligence that we unlock the capacity for true understanding, both within ourselves and in our shared world.

THE HUMAN SPECTRUM A GUIDING COMPASS
Navigating Emotions and Existence

The human experience is a vast and multifaceted landscape, a spectrum shimmering with the potential for profound connection, creativity, and self-discovery. Understanding this intricate landscape requires a synthesis of perspectives, drawing from the wisdom of humanism, the scientific rigor of psychology, and the practical application of emotional intelligence. These three domains, while distinct in their approaches, are inextricably linked, offering a holistic framework for comprehending the complexities of the human condition and fostering a world built on empathy, understanding, and flourishing.

Humanism, at its core, is a philosophy that celebrates the inherent worth and dignity of every individual. It emphasizes human agency, reason, and potential. It posits that we are not merely puppets of fate or deterministic forces, but rather active agents in shaping our own lives and contributing to the betterment of society. Humanistic psychology, born from this philosophical foundation, moves away from the deterministic views of behaviorism and psychoanalysis to focus on the subjective experience of the individual. Figures like Abraham Maslow and Carl Rogers championed the importance of self-actualization, the innate drive to reach one's full potential. They believed that given the right conditions – unconditional positive regard, empathy, and genuineness – individuals could overcome obstacles and achieve a fulfilling life.

This focus on individual agency and inherent goodness is particularly potent in a world often characterized by cynicism and despair. Humanism provides a beacon of hope, reminding us that despite our flaws and shortcomings, we possess the capacity for growth, compassion, and meaningful contribution. It encourages us to embrace our unique strengths and talents, to strive for excellence in all our endeavors, and to create a world that is more just, equitable, and compassionate for all. It underscores the importance of education, critical thinking, and ethical decision-making, empowering individuals to navigate the complexities of modern life with wisdom and integrity.

However, humanism, while inspiring, can sometimes be perceived as idealistic. It is here that the grounding perspective of psychology becomes crucial. Psychology, as a science, seeks to understand the human mind and behavior through empirical observation and experimentation. It delves into the intricacies of cognition, emotion, motivation, and social interaction, providing a framework for understanding the underlying mechanisms that drive our thoughts, feelings, and actions. From cognitive psychology, we learn about the biases and heuristics that can cloud our judgment; from developmental psychology, we gain insights into the stages of human growth and the factors that influence our development; and from social psychology, we understand the powerful influence of social context on our behavior.

Psychological research provides invaluable tools for understanding the challenges and complexities of the human experience. By studying mental health disorders, for example, we can develop effective treatments and interventions to alleviate suffering and promote well-being. By understanding the factors that contribute to prejudice and discrimination, we can develop strategies to promote tolerance and understanding. And by studying the principles of learning and motivation, we can create more effective educational programs and workplaces.

The marriage of humanism and psychology creates a powerful synergy. Humanism provides the ethical framework and the vision of human potential, while psychology provides the scientific tools and knowledge to understand how to achieve that potential. However, knowledge alone is not enough. To truly harness the power of humanism and psychology, we need to cultivate emotional intelligence.

Emotional intelligence (EQ) is the ability to understand and manage our own emotions, as well as the emotions of others. It encompasses a range of skills, including self-awareness, self-regulation, empathy, social skills, and motivation. EQ is not simply about being "nice" or avoiding conflict. It is about being aware of our emotional landscape and using that awareness to navigate complex social situations, build strong relationships, and make sound decisions.

In a world that is increasingly interconnected and complex, emotional intelligence is becoming an indispensable skill. It allows us to communicate effectively, resolve conflicts peacefully, and build trust with others. In the workplace, EQ is a critical factor in leadership effectiveness, team performance, and employee engagement. In our personal lives, EQ helps us build strong, fulfilling relationships and navigate the challenges of life with resilience and grace.

The development of emotional intelligence is a lifelong journey. It requires self-reflection, conscious effort, and a willingness to learn from our experiences. Practices like mindfulness meditation, journaling, and seeking feedback from others can help us become more aware of our emotions and how they impact our behavior. By cultivating empathy and practicing active listening, we can learn to understand the perspectives of others and build stronger connections.

The integration of humanism, psychology, and emotional intelligence offers a powerful framework for understanding and nurturing the human spectrum. Humanism reminds us of the inherent worth and potential of every individual. Psychology provides the scientific tools and knowledge to understand the complexities of the human mind and behavior. And emotional intelligence equips us with the skills to navigate the social world with empathy, understanding, and effectiveness.

Imagine a world where education is not just about acquiring knowledge, but also about developing emotional intelligence and fostering a sense of social responsibility. Imagine a workplace where leadership is based on empathy and collaboration, rather than power and control. Imagine a society where differences are celebrated, and everyone feels valued and respected. This is the vision that emerges from the synthesis of humanism, psychology, and emotional intelligence – a vision of a world where human potential is fully realized, and all individuals can thrive.

The journey towards this vision is not without its challenges. We live in a world filled with conflict, inequality, and environmental degradation. However, by embracing the principles of humanism, psychology, and emotional intelligence, we can create a more just, sustainable, and compassionate world for ourselves and for future generations. It requires a conscious effort to cultivate self-awareness, practice empathy, and act with integrity. It requires a commitment to lifelong learning and a willingness to challenge our own biases and assumptions.

Ultimately, understanding the human spectrum is about recognizing the inherent interconnectedness of all human beings. We are all part of a vast and complex web of relationships, and our actions have a profound impact on others. By embracing our shared humanity and cultivating our emotional intelligence, we can create a world where all individuals can flourish and reach their full potential, contributing to a vibrant and thriving human tapestry. This is not merely a utopian dream, but a tangible possibility, within reach if we choose to embrace the power of humanism, psychology, and emotional intelligence and weave them together into the fabric of our lives.

THE UNDAUNTED SPIRIT
A Humanist Call to Meaning, Empathy, and Action

Humanism, at its core, is a profound affirmation of the human experience. It is a philosophy that places humanity, with its inherent potential for reason, creativity, and compassion, at the center of its moral universe. It eschews reliance on supernatural beliefs in favor of ethical frameworks built upon evidence, empathy, and the unwavering pursuit of human flourishing. In a world often fragmented by dogma, driven by greed, and shadowed by despair, humanism offers a powerful and inspiring alternative, a call to action to embrace our shared humanity and build a more just, equitable, and meaningful world for all.

The philosophical foundation of humanism is rooted in the belief that we, as human beings, are capable of understanding the world through reason and observation. It is a rejection of blind faith and unquestioning obedience to authority, in favor of critical thinking, scientific inquiry, and the constant questioning of established norms. This embrace of reason is not simply an intellectual exercise; it is a vital tool for navigating the complexities of life, for discerning truth from falsehood, and for making informed decisions that benefit ourselves and the wider community. By trusting our intellect and embracing the power of knowledge, we can unravel the mysteries of the universe and unlock solutions to the challenges that confront us. This reliance on reason extends beyond the individual, advocating for evidence-based policies and rational discourse in the public sphere. In a world awash with misinformation and manipulated narratives, the humanist emphasis on critical thinking is more crucial than ever. It empowers individuals to be discerning consumers of information, to analyze claims with skepticism, and to resist the allure of simplistic solutions to complex problems. Furthermore, it compels us to constantly refine our understanding of the world, acknowledging that knowledge is ever-evolving and that our current beliefs may be subject to revision in light of new evidence.

However, humanism is not solely about intellect. It recognizes the crucial role of emotions, creativity, and imagination in shaping our understanding of the world and in enriching our lives. Art, music, literature, and human connection are not mere diversions; they are essential expressions of our humanity, fostering empathy, promoting understanding, and allowing us to connect with others on a deeper, more meaningful level. To be truly humanistic is to cultivate our capacity for wonder, to find beauty in the everyday, and to embrace the power of art to inspire, challenge, and transform. The creative arts provide a unique lens through which to explore the human condition, allowing us to grapple with complex emotions, contemplate existential questions, and imagine alternative possibilities for the future. They foster a sense of shared experience, transcending cultural and linguistic barriers to connect us through universal themes of love, loss, joy, and sorrow. In a world often dominated by utilitarian concerns, humanism reminds us of the intrinsic value of artistic expression and its vital role in enriching our lives and fostering a sense of community.

The inspiring power of humanism lies in its unwavering belief in the inherent worth and dignity of every individual. Regardless of race, religion, gender, sexual orientation, or any other arbitrary distinction, humanism asserts that all human beings are deserving of respect, compassion, and equal opportunities. This principle of universal human dignity is the bedrock of humanist ethics, guiding us to treat others with kindness, empathy, and understanding. It calls upon us to challenge injustice, fight against discrimination, and advocate for the rights and well-being of all, especially those who are marginalized or vulnerable. This commitment to universal dignity extends beyond our immediate circles, requiring us to consider the impact of our actions on individuals and communities around the globe. It compels us to be mindful of the interconnectedness of humanity and to recognize that the well-being of each individual is inextricably linked to the well-being of all.

This commitment to social justice is not merely a philosophical ideal; it is a call to action. Humanism compels us to actively engage in the world, to work towards creating a more just and equitable society. This can take many forms, from volunteering in our local communities to advocating for policy changes at the national level. It means standing up for the rights of the oppressed, challenging systemic inequalities, and working towards a future where all individuals have the opportunity to thrive. This active engagement necessitates a willingness to confront difficult truths about the injustices that persist in our societies. It requires us to be critical of the power structures that perpetuate inequality and to be actively involved in dismantling those structures. It also demands a commitment to lifelong learning, as we continually strive to understand the complex social, economic, and political forces that shape our world.

Furthermore, humanism recognizes the crucial importance of personal responsibility and ethical conduct. It acknowledges that we are all interconnected and that our actions have consequences, not only for ourselves but also for others and for the planet. This understanding of interconnectedness inspires us to act with integrity, honesty, and compassion in all our dealings. It encourages us to be mindful consumers, responsible citizens, and stewards of the environment. The concept of personal responsibility within humanism extends beyond simply avoiding harm to others. It also encompasses a proactive responsibility to contribute to the well-being of our communities and the preservation of the environment. This requires us to be informed and engaged citizens, actively participating in the democratic process and advocating for policies that promote social justice and environmental sustainability. It also necessitates a willingness to make personal sacrifices, such as reducing our consumption, supporting ethical businesses, and volunteering our time to worthy causes.

The motivational power of humanism stems from its capacity to provide meaning and purpose in a world that can often feel chaotic and meaningless. By embracing the humanist principles of reason, empathy, and social justice, we can create a life that is both fulfilling and impactful. We can find purpose in contributing to the well-being of others, in striving to create a more just and equitable world, and in leaving a positive legacy for future generations. In a world saturated with consumerism and fleeting pleasures, humanism offers a deeper and more enduring source of meaning and fulfillment. It encourages us to focus on intrinsic values such as personal growth, meaningful relationships, and contributing to the common good. By aligning our actions with our values, we can create a life that is characterized by purpose, integrity, and a sense of lasting satisfaction.

However, the humanist path is not without its challenges. It requires constant self-reflection, a willingness to question our own biases, and a commitment to continuous learning. It demands that we engage in difficult conversations, challenge established power structures, and stand up for what we believe in, even when it is unpopular or uncomfortable. This commitment to self-reflection and continuous learning is essential for navigating the complexities of the modern world. We must be willing to confront our own prejudices and biases, recognizing that we are all products of our upbringing and cultural context. We must also be open to new ideas and perspectives, engaging in respectful dialogue with those who hold different viewpoints. This process of self-discovery and intellectual growth is a lifelong journey, but it is essential for living a truly authentic and meaningful life.

Additionally, the humanist commitment to challenging established power structures can be met with resistance and even hostility. Standing up for justice and equality often requires us to confront powerful vested interests and challenge deeply ingrained social norms. This can be a difficult and even dangerous undertaking, but it is essential for creating a more just and equitable world. Humanists must be prepared to face criticism, ridicule, and even persecution for their beliefs. However, they must also be resilient and unwavering in their commitment to their principles, drawing strength from the knowledge that they are fighting for a better future for all.

In a world increasingly characterized by division and conflict, humanism offers a beacon of hope, a pathway towards a more unified and compassionate future. By embracing our shared humanity, by cultivating our capacity for reason and empathy, and by working together to build a more just and equitable world, we can create a future where all individuals have the opportunity to reach their full potential. This is the undaunted spirit of humanism – a call to meaning, empathy, and action that resonates deeply within the human heart, urging us to embrace our shared humanity and create a better world for ourselves and for generations to come. Let us answer that call with courage, compassion, and unwavering determination. The future of humanity depends on it. Let us remember, the pursuit of a better world is not a passive endeavor, but an active and ongoing commitment to the principles of humanism, a commitment that demands our constant engagement and unwavering dedication.

To nurture emotional intelligence is to plant seeds of understanding in the fertile ground of our interactions, to cultivate a climate where listening is an art, where silence is valued, and where the unspoken language of feelings is given the space to bloom, transforming our relationships into gardens of mutual respect and profound connection.

UNDERSTANDING HUMAN EMOTIONS
The Nature of Emotions

Emotions are intricate responses to stimuli that encompass a range of feelings, thoughts, and physiological changes. They serve as fundamental components of human experience, influencing behavior and shaping interpersonal relationships. At their core, emotions are adaptive mechanisms that evolved to enhance survival and foster social cohesion. They arise in reaction to external events or internal thoughts, providing individuals with critical information about their environment and their own psychological state. This interplay between cognition and emotion underscores the complexity of human experience and highlights the significance of understanding emotions within the framework of humanistic psychology.

Emotions, that vibrant, often tumultuous, symphony played upon the strings of our being, are the very essence of what it means to be human. They are the colors that paint our experiences, the wind that fills the sails of our motivations, the very ground from which our understanding of the world takes root. To understand the nature of emotions is not merely to dissect a biological process, but to embark on a profound philosophical journey, one that reveals the core of our existence, inspires us to navigate the complexities of life with greater awareness, and motivates us to cultivate a richer, more meaningful connection with ourselves and the world around us.

Philosophically, emotions have been debated for centuries, often relegated to the realm of irrationality, a counterpoint to the supposed purity of reason. Stoics championed the suppression of emotions, advocating for a life governed solely by logic and virtue. Yet, this perspective overlooks the inherent value and intricate complexity of human feeling. Emotions are not simply disturbances to be quelled, but rather powerful signals, evolved over millennia to guide our survival and enhance our social bonds. Fear alerts us to danger, joy celebrates success, grief allows us to process loss, and love binds us together in communities of support and growth. To deny these feelings is to deny a fundamental aspect of our being, to silence a vital voice that speaks of our needs, desires, and connections.

The nature of emotions, then, is far from simple. They are not just fleeting sensations, but complex, multifaceted phenomena interwoven with our thoughts, beliefs, and experiences. A single event can trigger a cascade of emotions, each influencing the other, creating a unique and nuanced response. The sting of betrayal, for instance, can ignite anger, fuel sadness, and sow the seeds of mistrust. Understanding this interconnectedness allows us to delve deeper into the roots of our emotional reactions, to identify the underlying beliefs and experiences that shape our responses. This self-awareness is not merely intellectual curiosity; it is a key to unlocking personal growth and fostering healthier relationships.

The recognition of emotions as valuable and complex opens the door to a more authentic and compassionate existence. By embracing our emotional landscape, we can learn to navigate its peaks and valleys with greater grace and resilience. When we allow ourselves to feel the full spectrum of human emotions, we become more attuned to the experiences of others. Empathy blossoms, allowing us to connect on a deeper level, to understand and share the burdens and joys of those around us. This compassionate understanding is the bedrock of strong relationships, thriving communities, and a more just and equitable world.

Imagine a world where we are all encouraged to explore and express our emotions openly and honestly. A world where vulnerability is seen not as a weakness, but as a strength, a testament to our capacity for empathy and connection. This is not a utopian fantasy, but a potential reality that we can actively cultivate. By challenging societal norms that discourage emotional expression, by creating safe spaces for sharing and processing our feelings, and by educating ourselves and others about the nature of emotions, we can pave the way for a more emotionally intelligent society.

Understanding the nature of emotions is profoundly motivational. It empowers us to take control of our emotional responses, to shape our experiences, and to live more fulfilling lives. We are not simply puppets of our emotions, tossed about by the whims of circumstance. We have the capacity to learn, to grow, and to develop strategies for managing our emotions effectively. This might involve practicing mindfulness, engaging in self-reflection, seeking therapy, or simply learning to identify and name our emotions as they arise.

By mastering our emotional intelligence, we can transform challenges into opportunities for growth. Fear, for example, can be transformed from a paralyzing force into a catalyst for courage. Grief can become a pathway to healing and renewed appreciation for life.

Anger, if channeled constructively, can be a powerful motivator for positive change. When we understand the underlying messages and potential benefits of our emotions, we can harness their energy to fuel our passions, pursue our goals, and make a meaningful contribution to the world.

Understanding the nature of human emotions is a journey of profound philosophical significance, offering inspiration and motivation for a richer, more meaningful existence. By embracing the full spectrum of our feelings, by cultivating emotional intelligence, and by fostering a culture of empathy and understanding, we can unlock our potential for personal growth, strengthen our relationships, and create a more compassionate world. Let us not shy away from the symphony of feeling, but rather embrace its complexity, learn from its wisdom, and allow it to guide us towards a life lived with greater awareness, purpose, and connection. For in understanding our emotions, we understand ourselves, and in understanding ourselves, we unlock the potential to create a truly harmonious and fulfilling existence.

The classification of emotions has been a subject of extensive research, with various theories proposing different models. One of the most widely recognized is Paul Ekman's model, which identifies six basic emotions: happiness, sadness, fear, anger, surprise, and disgust. These emotions are universal, transcending cultural boundaries and appearing in similar expressions across diverse populations. Such universality suggests that emotions are not only personal experiences but also collective phenomena that bind humanity together. By examining these basic emotions, we can gain insights into the human experience and the ways in which emotions shape our interactions and societal structures.

Emotions also play a critical role in motivation and decision-making. They can drive individuals toward or away from specific actions, influencing choices in personal, social, and professional contexts. For instance, feelings of joy can motivate people to pursue goals and engage positively with others, while fear may prompt caution and avoidance. This relationship between emotion and behavior underscores the importance of emotional awareness. Understanding one's own emotional responses and those of others can lead to more informed decision-making and healthier interpersonal dynamics, aligning closely with the principles of humanistic psychology that emphasize self-awareness and personal growth.

Moreover, the concept of emotional intelligence has emerged as a vital aspect of personal and professional development. Emotional intelligence refers to the ability to recognize, understand, and manage one's own emotions while empathizing with the emotions of others. This skill set fosters better communication, enhances relationships, and promotes mental well-being. In the context of humanistic psychology, emotional intelligence aligns with the idea of self-actualization, where individuals strive to reach their fullest potential through self-awareness and meaningful connections with others. By cultivating emotional intelligence, adults can navigate the complexities of their emotions and improve their quality of life.

The nature of emotions is multi-layered, encompassing biological, psychological, and social dimensions. As vital elements of the human experience, emotions influence our thoughts, actions, and relationships, providing essential insights into our existence. Understanding emotions through the lens of humanistic psychology not only enhances self-awareness but also fosters deeper connections with others. This exploration of emotions invites adults to reflect on their emotional experiences and encourages a journey toward greater emotional intelligence and fulfillment in life.

The Role of Emotions *in* Human Experience

Emotions play a crucial role in shaping human experience, serving as both a lens through which individuals interpret their surroundings and a catalyst for action. They are deeply embedded in the fabric of human existence, influencing thoughts, behaviors, and interpersonal relationships. Understanding emotions is essential not only for personal growth but also for fostering empathy and connection among individuals. Humanistic psychology emphasizes the significance of emotions in achieving self-actualization and understanding one's place within the larger tapestry of humanity.

At the core of human experience, emotions act as navigational tools that guide individuals through their lives. They signal needs and desires, shaping decisions and responses to various situations. Positive emotions, such as joy and love, often lead to nurturing behaviors, enhancing social bonds and promoting well-being. Conversely, negative emotions like fear and anger can serve protective functions, alerting individuals to potential threats and prompting necessary changes in their environment. This duality illustrates that all emotions, regardless of their perceived value, contribute to the richness of human experience.

Emotions are inherently social, influencing how individuals relate to one another. They facilitate communication and understanding, allowing individuals to express their inner states and connect with others on a deeper level. Emotional expression fosters intimacy and trust, essential components of healthy relationships. Humanistic psychology underscores the importance of this emotional sharing, viewing it as a pathway to greater self-awareness and authentic connections. In this way, emotions not only enrich individual lives but also strengthen the social fabric that binds communities together.

The interaction between emotions and cognition further complicates the human experience. Emotions can significantly affect thinking patterns, often leading to biases or distortions in judgment. A person in a state of anger may perceive situations more negatively, while someone experiencing happiness might overlook potential risks. Humanistic psychology encourages individuals to cultivate emotional intelligence, enabling them to recognize and manage their emotional responses effectively. This awareness fosters resilience, empowering individuals to navigate life's complexities with greater clarity and purpose.

The exploration of emotions is integral to understanding what it means to be human. By acknowledging the multifaceted role emotions play in shaping experiences, individuals can embark on a journey of self-discovery and personal growth. Humanistic psychology advocates for embracing the full spectrum of emotions as a means to enhance one's existence, promoting a life characterized by authenticity, empathy, and connection. In recognizing the profound impact of emotions, individuals can better appreciate their shared humanity and the intricate web of experiences that define the human condition.

Emotional Intelligence *and its* Importance

Emotional intelligence (EI) encompasses the ability to recognize, understand, and manage our own emotions while also being attuned to the emotions of others. This multifaceted skill set plays a crucial role in our interpersonal relationships, decision-making processes, and overall mental health. Unlike traditional intelligence, which is often measured through cognitive abilities, emotional intelligence involves a deeper understanding of emotional dynamics, enabling individuals to navigate the complexities of human interactions. As society increasingly values emotional well-being, the significance of EI becomes more pronounced, influencing both personal and professional realms.

The importance of emotional intelligence can be observed in various contexts, particularly in the workplace. Organizations that prioritize EI often experience improved communication, collaboration, and conflict resolution among team members. Employees with high emotional intelligence are adept at recognizing their own emotional triggers and can manage stress effectively, leading to enhanced productivity and job satisfaction. Furthermore, leaders who exhibit strong emotional intelligence inspire trust and loyalty, fostering a positive organizational culture.

This highlights how emotional intelligence is not merely an individual trait but a vital component of collective success in any community.

In personal relationships, emotional intelligence serves as a cornerstone for building empathy and understanding. Individuals who are emotionally intelligent can better navigate the intricacies of their relationships, responding to the needs and feelings of others with sensitivity. This capacity for empathy enables deeper connections, reducing misunderstandings and conflicts. By cultivating EI, individuals can enhance their ability to listen actively and communicate effectively, leading to healthier, more fulfilling interpersonal dynamics. As a result, emotional intelligence is essential for sustaining long-term relationships, whether they be familial, platonic, or romantic.

Emotional intelligence has profound implications for mental health. Individuals with high levels of EI tend to have better coping strategies when faced with stress, anxiety, or depression. By recognizing their emotional states, they can implement healthy coping mechanisms, such as mindfulness practices or seeking social support. This self-awareness not only aids in personal growth but also contributes to resilience in the face of adversity. As mental health awareness continues to grow, the role of emotional intelligence in promoting psychological well-being cannot be overstated, emphasizing its importance in fostering a balanced and fulfilling life.

Finally, emotional intelligence is a vital aspect of the human experience, shaping our interactions, relationships, and mental health. Its significance extends beyond individual benefits, influencing organizational effectiveness and societal cohesion. By understanding and developing emotional intelligence, adults can enhance their ability to connect with others, navigate challenges, and cultivate a greater sense of empathy. As we continue to explore the depths of human existence, acknowledging the importance of emotional intelligence becomes essential in our journey toward greater self-awareness and collective harmony.

THE SPECTRUM OF HUMAN EXPERIENCE
Defining the Human Spectrum

Defining the Human Spectrum involves understanding the diverse range of human experiences, emotions, and behaviors that shape our existence. Humanistic psychology emphasizes the importance of individual perspective and the subjective experience of each person. This approach posits that every individual exists on a spectrum that includes a vast array of emotions, motivations, and personal narratives. By recognizing this spectrum, we can appreciate the complexity of human experience and the significance of each person's unique story.

At the core of the human spectrum is the interplay between emotional states and cognitive processes. Emotions serve as fundamental signals that inform individuals about their internal states and external environments. They can range from joy and love to sadness and anger, creating a rich tapestry of feelings that influence decision-making and interpersonal relationships. Understanding these emotions helps individuals navigate their own lives and fosters empathy towards others, as we recognize that everyone experiences similar feelings, albeit in different intensities and contexts.

Another critical aspect of the human spectrum is the consideration of developmental stages and cultural influences. Humanistic psychology acknowledges that our experiences are shaped not only by individual choices but also by societal expectations and cultural backgrounds. Each stage of life—from childhood to old age—brings unique challenges and opportunities for growth. Additionally, cultural narratives inform the way emotions are expressed and understood, leading to a diverse range of emotional expressions across different societies. This intersection of personal and collective experiences contributes to a broader understanding of humanity.

The human spectrum also encompasses the notion of existential crises and the search for meaning. As individuals confront their mortality and the complexities of existence, they often grapple with questions of purpose and identity. These existential dilemmas can lead to profound emotional experiences, ranging from despair to enlightenment. Humanistic psychology encourages individuals to explore these crises as opportunities for personal growth, promoting self-awareness and a deeper understanding of one's own place within the broader human experience.

Defining the human spectrum is an essential endeavor that highlights the richness of human emotions, the impact of cultural contexts, and the significance of existential exploration. By embracing this spectrum, individuals can cultivate a greater appreciation for their own experiences and those of others. This understanding fosters connection, empathy, and a shared sense of humanity, allowing us to navigate the complexities of our emotions and existence with greater awareness and compassion.

The Intersection *of* Emotions *and* Existence

Existence, in its rawest form, is a daunting prospect: a vast, echoing void punctuated by the fleeting moments of experience. Yet, within that void, something blooms, something vibrant and undeniably human – emotion. It is at the intersection of these two seemingly disparate forces, existence and emotion, that we find not just life, but a life imbued with meaning, purpose, and the potential for transcendence. Emotions are not merely reactions to external stimuli, but rather the very threads that weave the tapestry of our existence, shaping our perceptions, driving our actions, and ultimately defining what it means to be human.

Philosophically, the relationship between emotions and existence has been a subject of profound contemplation for centuries. Existentialists like Sartre argued that existence precedes essence.

We are born into the world without inherent meaning, and it is through our choices, fueled by our emotions, that we forge our own identity.

The feeling of angst, the weight of responsibility for our own being, is a cornerstone of this philosophy. It is the recognition that we are free to choose, and that this freedom, paradoxically, is both terrifying and empowering.

Emotions, therefore, are not obstacles to overcome, but rather the compass guiding us through the labyrinth of existence. They are the visceral indicators that alert us to the significance of our choices, the consequences of our actions, and the potential for living authentically.

Consider the emotion of grief. When faced with loss, we are confronted with the stark reality of our mortality and the impermanence of all things. It is a painful, overwhelming experience that can shake the very foundations of our being. Yet, within grief lies the potential for profound growth. It forces us to confront our vulnerability, to examine our values, and to appreciate the preciousness of the relationships we hold dear. The tears shed in mourning are not merely expressions of sadness, but also a cleansing of the soul, allowing us to emerge from the darkness with a renewed appreciation for life.

Similarly, the emotion of joy is not simply a fleeting moment of happiness, but a testament to our capacity for connection, love, and meaning. It is the feeling of being fully alive, of being connected to something larger than ourselves, whether it be through art, nature, or human connection. Joy reminds us of the beauty and wonder that exists in the world, even amidst the chaos and suffering. It fuels our creativity, inspires our actions, and encourages us to seek out experiences that resonate with our deepest values.

Inspirational narratives are replete with examples of individuals who have harnessed the power of their emotions to overcome incredible obstacles and achieve remarkable feats. Nelson Mandela, imprisoned for 27 years, transformed his anger and resentment into forgiveness and compassion, ultimately leading to the dismantling of apartheid in South Africa. His story is a testament to the transformative power of emotions when channeled with purpose and directed towards a higher ideal. He understood that allowing his negative emotions to consume him would only perpetuate the cycle of violence and oppression. Instead, he chose to cultivate empathy and understanding, creating a path towards reconciliation and healing.

Emotions are intrinsically linked to creativity and innovation. Artists, writers, and musicians often draw inspiration from their own emotional experiences, translating feelings of love, loss, anger, and joy into works of art that resonate deeply with audiences.

The raw emotion expressed in Van Gogh's paintings, the poignant lyrics of Leonard Cohen's songs, and the powerful social commentary of Toni Morrison's novels are all examples of how emotions can fuel creative expression and contribute to a richer understanding of the human condition. By embracing our emotional landscape, we unlock our creative potential and contribute to the cultural tapestry of humanity.

Motivational speakers often emphasize the importance of tapping into our emotions to achieve our goals. They encourage us to identify our passions, to connect with our purpose, and to cultivate a sense of unwavering belief in our own abilities. This is not about suppressing negative emotions, but rather about harnessing the power of positive emotions to drive us forward, even in the face of adversity. The feeling of excitement when pursuing a challenging goal, the satisfaction of overcoming obstacles, and the deep sense of fulfillment that comes from contributing to something meaningful are all powerful motivators that can propel us toward success and a more fulfilling existence.

However, it is crucial to acknowledge that emotions can also be destructive. Uncontrolled anger can lead to violence, unchecked fear can lead to paralysis, and overwhelming sadness can lead to despair. The key lies in developing emotional intelligence, the ability to understand and manage our own emotions, as well as the emotions of others. This involves cultivating self-awareness, practicing empathy, and developing healthy coping mechanisms for dealing with difficult emotions. It requires a conscious effort to understand the root causes of our emotions, to challenge negative thought patterns, and to cultivate a more balanced and compassionate perspective.

The intersection of emotions and existence is a complex and multifaceted phenomenon. It is a constant dance between feeling and being, between reacting and responding, between embracing the chaos and seeking meaning in the void. By understanding the power and potential of our emotions, we can navigate the complexities of existence with greater awareness, resilience, and purpose. We can choose to cultivate positive emotions, to learn from our negative emotions, and to harness the power of both to create a life that is both meaningful and fulfilling.

The intersection of emotions and existence invites deep exploration, particularly within the context of humanistic psychology. This field emphasizes the inherent value of human beings and their capacity for self-actualization, suggesting that emotions serve as a critical bridge between one's inner self and the external world. Emotions are not merely reactions to stimuli; they are integral components of our existence that shape our perceptions, influence our decisions, and ultimately define our humanity. Understanding this intersection can illuminate how we navigate our experiences, relationships, and personal growth.

At the core of humanistic psychology lies the belief that individuals possess the agency to shape their lives and meanings. Emotions act as the compass guiding this journey. When a person experiences joy, for instance, it often propels them toward authentic connections and meaningful experiences. Conversely, emotions like fear and sadness can signal the need for introspection and change. This dynamic interplay underscores the importance of emotional awareness, as recognizing and understanding one's feelings can lead to greater self-acceptance and a more profound understanding of one's place in the world.

Existence itself is often fraught with uncertainty and ambiguity, making the role of emotions even more significant. In moments of crisis or existential doubt, emotions can serve as both a source of distress and a pathway to clarity. They prompt individuals to confront uncomfortable truths about themselves and their circumstances. This confrontation can catalyze personal growth and transformation, as individuals learn to embrace the full spectrum of their emotional experiences. Thus, navigating the complexities of existence becomes a process of emotional exploration, allowing for a richer, more nuanced understanding of the self.

The intersection of emotions and existence reveals the interconnectedness of individuals within a broader social context. Our emotional experiences are often influenced by our relationships, cultural backgrounds, and societal norms. Humanistic psychology emphasizes the importance of empathy and understanding in fostering emotional well-being. By cultivating emotional intelligence, individuals can enhance their capacity for compassion, both toward themselves and others. This interconnectedness not only deepens personal relationships but also contributes to a more harmonious society, where emotional expression is valued and understood.

Examining the intersection of emotions and existence offers invaluable insights into the human experience. Emotions are not just fleeting feelings; they are foundational to our understanding of ourselves and our relationships with others. By embracing this intersection, individuals can navigate life's challenges with greater resilience and authenticity. The insights gained from this exploration underscore the essence of humanity, highlighting how our emotional landscape shapes our existence and ultimately defines who we are in this intricate tapestry of life.

Therefore, let us embrace the full spectrum of our emotional experiences, not as obstacles to overcome, but as essential threads in the fabric of our existence. Let us learn to listen to the whispers of our hearts, to trust the wisdom of our intuition, and to cultivate a deep sense of compassion for ourselves and for others. For it is in the profound essence of our emotions that we find the true meaning of life, the potential for transcendence, and the enduring beauty of the human spirit. Let us weave a legacy worthy of the gift of existence, a heritage filled with love, joy, compassion, and the unwavering pursuit of a life lived authentically and with purpose.

Cultural Influences *on* Emotional Expression

Cultural influences significantly shape how individuals express their emotions, dictating the acceptable modes of emotional expression and the contexts in which they occur. Different cultures possess unique emotional norms and values, which can affect everything from facial expressions to gestures and verbal communication. For example, in many Western cultures, overt displays of emotion such as crying or shouting may be more socially acceptable, whereas in some Eastern cultures, emotional restraint is often valued as a sign of wisdom and self-control. Understanding these cultural variations is essential for grasping the complexities of human emotional expression.

Language plays a crucial role in cultural influences on emotional expression. The vocabulary available in a particular language can shape how emotions are experienced and communicated. For instance, some cultures have specific words to describe emotions that may not have direct equivalents in other languages, leading to a richer emotional landscape within those societies. The Sapir-Whorf hypothesis suggests that language influences thought, which in turn implies that the nuances of emotional experience can be profoundly affected by linguistic structures. This phenomenon highlights the importance of language as a cultural tool for emotional articulation.

Socialization processes within diverse cultures also dictate how individuals learn to manage and express their emotions. From childhood, individuals are taught what is appropriate and inappropriate in terms of emotional expression through family dynamics, community interactions, and societal expectations. For instance, in collectivist societies, individuals may prioritize group harmony over personal expression, leading to a suppression of individual emotional needs for the sake of social cohesion. Conversely, in individualistic cultures, there may be a greater emphasis on personal authenticity and self-expression, which can encourage more open emotional displays.

Rituals and traditions are another vital aspect of cultural influence on emotional expression. Many cultures have established rituals for expressing emotions during significant life events such as births, deaths, and weddings. These rituals provide a structured framework for individuals to express their feelings in a socially sanctioned manner. They can also facilitate communal experiences of emotion, fostering a sense of belonging and shared understanding among participants. The emotional weight carried by these rituals often transcends individual experiences, linking personal emotions to collective cultural narratives.

Globalization and cultural exchange have introduced new dynamics in emotional expression. As individuals encounter different cultural norms through travel, media, and migration, they may adopt or adapt various emotional expressions from other cultures. This blending of emotional expressions can lead to a richer, more diverse emotional experience but may also result in conflicts or misunderstandings when different cultural values clash. Navigating these complexities requires a sensitivity to the cultural backgrounds of others and an awareness of how one's own cultural influences shape emotional experiences. Understanding these cultural dimensions can enhance empathy and communication, ultimately enriching human connections.

The human heart, a delicate yet resilient vessel, holds within its chambers the vast universe of our emotional experiences, each feeling a celestial body, a star that illuminates the hidden corners of our consciousness, guiding us through the darkness of despair and the brilliance of joy, reminding us of the profound interconnectedness of all things.

HUMANISTIC PSYCHOLOGY FOUNDATIONS
Humanistic Psychology *as a* Beacon for Education *and* Self-Discovery

Humanistic psychology, a vibrant and often overlooked branch of psychological thought, offers a profound and deeply inspiring lens through which to understand the human experience and, crucially, to revolutionize education. More than a mere therapeutic approach, it is a philosophy of life, a motivational powerhouse, and a foundation for an educational system that truly empowers individuals to realize their full potential. This essay will explore the philosophical underpinnings of humanistic psychology, highlighting its core principles, its inspiring vision of human nature, and its potential to transform education into a journey of authentic self-discovery.

At its heart, humanistic psychology is a rejection of the deterministic views that characterize both psychoanalysis and behaviorism. While acknowledging the influence of biological drives and environmental conditioning, humanistic thinkers posit that humans are fundamentally free, rational, and inherently good, possessing an innate drive towards self-actualization: the realization of one's unique potential and the fulfillment of one's deepest aspirations. This optimism about human nature is not naive; it acknowledges the capacity for negativity and destructiveness but attributes these aberrations to societal and psychological impediments that stifle the inherent human potential for growth. The philosophical roots of this optimistic view can be traced to existentialism, which emphasizes individual freedom, responsibility, and the search for meaning in a seemingly absurd world, and to phenomenology, which highlights the importance of subjective experience in understanding reality. This grounding in existential and phenomenological thought infuses humanistic psychology with a profound respect for the individual's unique journey and the inherent value in their lived experience, a stark contrast to the often reductionist approaches of other psychological schools.

This focus on subjective experience is paramount. Humanistic psychology insists that understanding a person requires empathy, deep listening, and a genuine attempt to see the world through their eyes. This emphasis on empathy is profoundly inspiring, reminding us that each individual is a universe unto themselves, worthy of respect and understanding. The core concepts of Rogers' Person-Centered Therapy, such as unconditional positive regard, congruence (genuineness), and empathetic understanding, provide practical tools for fostering authentic relationships and creating environments where individuals feel safe to explore their inner landscape. These concepts are not just applicable in therapy; they are fundamental principles for building strong, supportive communities and for cultivating meaningful relationships in all aspects of life. Imagine the transformative power of applying unconditional positive regard, not just to troubled individuals, but to students struggling with academic or social challenges. Instead of focusing solely on correcting deficits, educators, guided by humanistic principles, would prioritize creating a safe space for vulnerability and growth, fostering self-acceptance and resilience.

Maslow's Hierarchy of Needs further illuminates this path towards self-actualization. He proposed that humans are motivated by a hierarchy of needs, beginning with basic physiological needs and progressing through safety, belonging and love, esteem, and finally, self-actualization. While the specific order and universality of this hierarchy have been debated, the underlying concept remains incredibly motivational. It suggests that individuals must first have their basic needs met before they can fully focus on personal growth and the pursuit of higher values. This understanding helps us to recognize the impact of social and economic inequalities on individual well-being and motivates us to create a more just and equitable society where everyone has the opportunity to thrive. Furthermore, Maslow's work highlights the importance of creating environments that foster a sense of security and belonging. A student who feels unsafe or unloved will struggle to focus on learning and self-discovery. Education, therefore, must extend beyond academics to address the emotional and social needs of students, creating a nurturing environment where they feel valued, respected, and connected.

The implications for education are transformative. Traditional education, often characterized by rote learning, standardized testing, and a focus on external rewards, can stifle creativity, critical thinking, and intrinsic motivation. Humanistic psychology provides an alternative vision: an education that is centered on the student, fostering their inherent curiosity, promoting their personal growth, and empowering them to become self-directed learners. This shift requires a fundamental re-evaluation of the purpose of education. Is it simply to prepare students for the workforce, or is it to cultivate well-rounded, self-aware individuals who are equipped to navigate the complexities of life and contribute meaningfully to society? Humanistic education champions the latter, prioritizing the development of the whole person – intellectually, emotionally, socially, and ethically.

Imagine an educational system where:

Learning is Passion-Driven: Curriculum is designed to ignite curiosity and allow students to explore their interests in depth. Subject matter is connected to real-world problems and opportunities, making learning relevant and engaging. Students are given choices and autonomy in their learning, fostering a sense of ownership and responsibility. This might involve project-based learning where students choose a topic related to a broader curriculum goal and then research, design, and present their findings in a way that reflects their individual strengths and interests. Furthermore, it could involve incorporating student voice into curriculum development through surveys and focus groups, ensuring that the learning experiences are relevant and engaging for the students they are designed to serve.

Empathy and Connection are Prioritized: Classrooms are spaces of trust and belonging, where students feel safe to express themselves, take risks, and learn from their mistakes. Teachers act as facilitators, guiding students on their learning journeys and fostering a sense of community. Collaborative projects and discussions are used to promote empathy, understanding, and respect for diverse perspectives. Implementing restorative justice practices, where students take responsibility for their actions and work to repair harm caused, can foster a culture of accountability and empathy. Furthermore, incorporating social-emotional learning (SEL) programs into the curriculum can equip students with the skills they need to navigate complex social situations, manage their emotions, and build positive relationships.

Creativity and Critical Thinking are Cultivated: Students are encouraged to think outside the box, to question assumptions, and to develop their own unique solutions to problems. Arts integration is used to stimulate creativity and imagination. Students are taught to analyze information critically and to form their own well-reasoned opinions. Encouraging debate and Socratic seminars allows students to engage in critical thinking and articulate their perspectives in a structured and respectful environment. Providing opportunities for students to design and conduct their own research projects allows them to develop critical thinking skills and learn how to evaluate information objectively.

Self-Reflection and Personal Growth are Encouraged: Students are given opportunities to reflect on their learning experiences, to identify their strengths and weaknesses, and to set goals for personal growth. Mindfulness practices and emotional intelligence training are incorporated into the curriculum. Students are encouraged to develop a strong sense of self-awareness and to live authentically. Journaling prompts that encourage self-reflection, such as "What did I learn today?" or "What am I grateful for?" can help students develop a deeper understanding of themselves and their experiences. Providing opportunities for students to participate in extracurricular activities and community service projects can help them discover their passions and develop a sense of purpose.

Assessment is Holistic and Individualized: The focus shifts from standardized testing to authentic assessment methods that measure students' understanding, skills, and personal growth. Portfolios, projects, and performance-based assessments are used to showcase students' achievements and to provide valuable feedback for improvement. Replacing high-stakes standardized tests with more authentic assessments that measure students' ability to apply their knowledge and skills in real-world contexts can provide a more accurate picture of their learning. Providing individualized feedback that focuses on specific strengths and areas for improvement can help students develop a growth mindset and take ownership of their learning.

Such an education empowers individuals not just to accumulate knowledge, but to become lifelong learners, critical thinkers, creative problem-solvers, and compassionate citizens. It fosters in them a deep sense of purpose and motivates them to contribute meaningfully to the world. It helps them to tap into their innate potential and to live lives that are both fulfilling and impactful. Implementing humanistic principles in education is not merely a pedagogical adjustment; it is a paradigm shift that prioritizes the holistic development of the individual, nurturing their potential to become authentic, engaged, and contributing members of society. This requires a commitment from educators, policymakers, and the community as a whole to invest in creating learning environments that are supportive, empowering, and conducive to self-discovery. Only then can we truly unlock the transformative power of humanistic psychology and create an educational system that serves as a beacon for individuals seeking to realize their full potential and make a positive difference in the world.

HISTORICAL CONTEXT *and* Key Figures

The historical context of humanistic psychology is rooted in a reaction against the deterministic views of behaviorism and psychoanalysis. In the mid-20th century, a group of psychologists began to advocate for a more holistic understanding of human experience, emphasizing the importance of personal agency, creativity, and the inherent potential for growth. This movement emerged during a time of significant social upheaval, marked by the civil rights movement, the counterculture of the 1960s, and a growing interest in self-actualization. These societal shifts provided fertile ground for a psychological approach that prioritized the subjective experience of individuals and their capacity for self-determination.

Key figures in the development of humanistic psychology include Abraham Maslow, Carl Rogers, and Rollo May. Maslow is best known for his hierarchy of needs, which outlines a progression of human motivation from basic physiological needs to the pursuit of self-actualization. His work emphasized the importance of personal growth and the potential within every individual to achieve their fullest potential. Carl Rogers, another pivotal figure, introduced the concept of client-centered therapy, which focused on creating a supportive therapeutic environment that fosters personal insight and self-acceptance. Rogers believed that individuals possess an innate drive towards self-improvement and that therapy should facilitate this process.

Rollo May brought an existential perspective to humanistic psychology, emphasizing the significance of individual experience and the search for meaning in life. He explored themes such as anxiety, freedom, and the human condition, arguing that confronting existential concerns is essential for personal development. May's work helped bridge the gap between humanistic and existential psychology, highlighting the importance of understanding the human experience in its entirety, including both the joys and the struggles inherent in existence. His contributions have been influential in shaping a more comprehensive understanding of human emotions and motivations.

The historical context of humanistic psychology also reflects broader philosophical influences, including existentialism and phenomenology. These philosophical traditions emphasize the importance of individual experience and the subjective nature of reality, which align closely with the principles of humanistic psychology. The integration of these ideas helped to create a framework that values personal meaning and emotional depth, allowing for a more nuanced understanding of human behavior and relationships. This philosophical grounding has encouraged psychologists and therapists to explore not just the mechanics of behavior, but the richness of human experience.

In conclusion, the evolution of humanistic psychology is anchored in a rich historical context and shaped by key figures who challenged prevailing psychological paradigms. Their contributions have fostered a deeper understanding of emotions, existence, and the essence of humanity. By emphasizing the importance of personal agency, self-actualization, and the search for meaning, humanistic psychology continues to resonate with individuals seeking to navigate the complexities of their emotional lives and understand their place within the broader spectrum of human existence.

CORE PRINCIPLES
of Humanistic Psychology

Humanistic psychology emerged as a response to the limitations of behaviorism and psychoanalysis, emphasizing a more holistic approach to understanding human experience. Central to this movement are several core principles that guide its philosophy and practice. At the heart of humanistic psychology is the belief in the inherent goodness of individuals and their potential for personal growth. This optimistic view posits that every person has the capacity for self-actualization, a process of realizing and fulfilling one's potential. Rather than focusing solely on pathology, humanistic psychologists prioritize understanding the whole person, taking into account their experiences, feelings, and aspirations.

Another fundamental principle is the emphasis on subjective experience. Humanistic psychology asserts that each individual's perspective is valid and worthy of exploration. This focus on personal experience allows therapists to foster an empathetic and accepting environment, where clients feel safe to express their thoughts and emotions. The therapeutic relationship is characterized by authenticity, empathy, and unconditional positive regard, which are essential for facilitating personal growth and self-discovery. By valuing the unique experiences of individuals, humanistic psychology encourages a deeper understanding of the self and how it relates to the world.

Self-awareness and personal responsibility are also critical components of humanistic psychology. This approach encourages individuals to take ownership of their thoughts, feelings, and actions, promoting a sense of agency in shaping their lives. By fostering self-awareness, individuals can better understand their motivations and the impact of their choices on their well-being. This principle aligns with the idea that personal growth is an ongoing process, requiring individuals to engage actively in their journey toward self-improvement and fulfillment. Humanistic psychologists guide clients in recognizing their strengths and abilities, helping them to navigate challenges with resilience and confidence.

The principle of holistic understanding underscores the importance of considering the individual within their broader context. Humanistic psychology advocates for a comprehensive approach that integrates emotional, cognitive, physical, and social dimensions of human experience. This perspective recognizes that individuals do not exist in isolation but are influenced by their relationships, culture, and environment. By acknowledging the interconnectedness of various aspects of life, humanistic psychologists can better support clients in addressing the complexities of their existence and enhancing their overall quality of life.

Lastly, the focus on human potential and creativity distinguishes humanistic psychology from other psychological frameworks. This approach celebrates the unique capacities of individuals to innovate, create, and experience joy. Humanistic psychologists encourage clients to explore their creativity and engage in activities that bring fulfillment and meaning. By nurturing this creative spirit, individuals can discover deeper insights about themselves and the world around them. Ultimately, the core principles of humanistic psychology serve as a guiding framework for understanding and supporting the essence of humanity, fostering a journey toward self-actualization and a richer emotional existence.

The Therapeutic Relationship *and* Its Impact

The therapeutic relationship is a cornerstone of humanistic psychology, representing a unique and powerful bond between therapist and client. This relationship is characterized by empathy, authenticity, and unconditional positive regard, which create a safe environment for individuals to explore their emotions and experiences. The quality of this relationship significantly influences the therapeutic process, as clients are more likely to engage deeply and authentically when they feel understood and accepted. The therapist's ability to connect on a personal level fosters trust, allowing clients to lower their defenses and delve into the complexities of their inner worlds.

Empathy plays a crucial role in shaping the therapeutic relationship. When therapists actively listen and strive to understand clients' perspectives, they validate their feelings and experiences. This empathetic engagement not only helps clients feel seen and heard but also empowers them to confront and process difficult emotions. Research has shown that a strong empathetic connection can lead to more positive therapeutic outcomes, as clients are more motivated to participate in their healing journey. This emotional attunement facilitates a deeper exploration of issues, promoting insights that might not emerge in less supportive environments.

Authenticity in the therapeutic relationship is equally important. Clients benefit when therapists openly share their thoughts and feelings, provided that such disclosures are appropriate and serve the client's best interests. This genuine interaction humanizes the therapist, making them more relatable and approachable. As clients witness their therapist's vulnerability, they may feel encouraged to express their own vulnerabilities, ultimately enhancing the depth of the therapeutic dialogue. This reciprocal honesty fosters a collaborative spirit and enhances the overall effectiveness of the therapeutic process.

Unconditional positive regard is another fundamental aspect of the therapeutic relationship. By accepting clients without judgment, therapists create a nurturing space where individuals can explore their feelings without fear of criticism. This acceptance allows clients to embrace their true selves, facilitating self-discovery and personal growth. When clients experience this nonjudgmental support, they are more likely to confront their inner conflicts and engage in meaningful self-reflection. The therapeutic space becomes a sanctuary for exploring identity, values, and existential concerns, promoting a sense of empowerment and agency.

The therapeutic relationship serves as a microcosm of human connection, reflecting the essential elements of empathy, authenticity, and acceptance. These elements not only enhance the therapeutic process but also mirror the fundamental needs we all have for connection and understanding in our lives. By fostering such relationships, both therapists and clients contribute to a greater understanding of the human experience. As individuals navigate their emotions and existence, the therapeutic relationship stands as a testament to the profound impact of genuine human connection on personal growth and healing.

Emotional intelligence is the quiet revolution of the heart, a movement that seeks to dismantle the structures of emotional ignorance and replace them with the pillars of empathy, understanding, and compassion, creating a society where the language of feelings is not a source of division, but a bridge to unity.

THE JOURNEY OF SELF ACTUALIZATION
THE ASCENT TO SELF

A Philosophical Journey *of* Self-Actualization

The human spirit, a restless explorer at its core, embarks on a lifelong journey to understand itself, to realize its potential, and to contribute meaningfully to the world. This quest, often fraught with challenges and uncertainties, culminates in the profound and elusive state of being known as self-actualization. The concept, popularized by Abraham Maslow, represents the fulfillment of one's deepest potential, a realization of unique talents and a connection to something larger than oneself. However, self-actualization is not a destination, but rather an ongoing process – a continuous unfolding of the individual, driven by intrinsic motivation and guided by a commitment to personal growth and authentic living. To delve into the journey of self-actualization is to contemplate the fundamental questions of human existence, to examine the nature of motivation, and to ultimately inspire a more meaningful and purposeful life.

Philosophically, self-actualization speaks to the very essence of human potentiality. Ancient thinkers, from Aristotle to Confucius, explored the idea of living a "good life," emphasizing the cultivation of virtues and the pursuit of excellence. Maslow's concept builds upon this foundation, proposing that each individual possesses an innate drive to become the best version of themselves. This inherent potentiality, however, often lies dormant, obscured by societal pressures, learned limitations, and the pursuit of external validation. Unlocking this potential requires a conscious effort to dismantle these barriers and to embrace the authentic self. It demands a willingness to question conventional wisdom, to challenge limiting beliefs, and to cultivate a deep understanding of one's own values and aspirations.

The journey towards self-actualization is inherently challenging. It requires navigating Maslow's hierarchy of needs, starting with the most basic physiological requirements and ascending through safety, love and belonging, and esteem needs before reaching the pinnacle of self-actualization. These lower-level needs must be reasonably satisfied before an individual can truly focus on personal growth and self-expression. Poverty, insecurity, and social isolation can all hinder the journey, diverting energies towards mere survival and hindering the exploration of higher potential. This highlights the importance of a supportive and nurturing environment, both internal and external, in fostering the conditions necessary for self-actualization.

The concept of motivation plays a crucial role in understanding the dynamics of this journey. Maslow distinguished between deficiency motivation and growth motivation. Deficiency motivation is driven by a lack or need — the desire to satisfy hunger, security, or social acceptance. While essential for survival, these motivations are ultimately limiting, as they focus on filling gaps rather than expanding possibilities. Growth motivation, on the other hand, stems from a deep-seated desire to learn, to create, to contribute, and to become more fully oneself. It is intrinsically driven, fueled by curiosity, passion, and a sense of purpose. Shifting from deficiency motivation to growth motivation is a key step in the journey of self-actualization, requiring a conscious effort to cultivate intrinsic desires and to prioritize personal growth over external rewards.

The inspiring aspect of self-actualization lies in its emphasis on individual uniqueness and the power of human potential. Self-actualized individuals are not defined by conformity or societal expectations, but rather by their own unique talents, passions, and values. They are creative, spontaneous, and accepting of themselves and others. They are problem-centered rather than self-centered, and they possess a deep sense of purpose that guides their actions. They are not perfect, but they are authentic, embracing both their strengths and their imperfections. This acceptance allows them to live with greater joy, resilience, and a profound sense of meaning.

The motivational force of self-actualization stems from its promise of a more fulfilling and purposeful life. While the journey is challenging, the rewards are immeasurable. By embracing our potential, we can experience a deeper sense of self-worth, stronger relationships, and a greater connection to the world around us. We can contribute our unique talents to society, making a positive impact and leaving a lasting legacy. Self-actualization is not about achieving fame or fortune, but rather about living in alignment with our values, pursuing our passions, and contributing to the well-being of ourselves and others.

Education, in its truest sense, plays a pivotal role in facilitating the journey of self-actualization. It is not simply about acquiring knowledge and skills, but about cultivating critical thinking, creativity, and self-awareness. A holistic education encourages students to explore their interests, to develop their talents, and to discover their purpose. It fosters a love of learning, a spirit of inquiry, and a commitment to personal growth. It empowers individuals to challenge conventional wisdom, to think for themselves, and to make informed decisions that align with their values. Furthermore, education can provide access to diverse perspectives, broadening our understanding of the world and helping us to develop empathy and compassion.

Teachers, as guides and mentors, have a profound responsibility to support students on their journey of self-actualization. By creating a supportive and nurturing learning environment, they can encourage students to take risks, to experiment with new ideas, and to express themselves authentically. They can also help students to identify their strengths, to develop their talents, and to discover their passions. By fostering a growth mindset, they can empower students to overcome challenges, to learn from their mistakes, and to continuously strive for improvement. Ultimately, the goal of education should be to empower students to become self-directed learners, capable of navigating the complexities of life and pursuing their own unique paths to self-actualization.

The journey of self-actualization is a lifelong pursuit of personal growth, authenticity, and purpose. It is a philosophical quest to understand the nature of human potential, a motivational force that drives us to become the best versions of ourselves, and an educational imperative that empowers us to live more meaningful and fulfilling lives. While the path is often challenging, the rewards are immeasurable. By embracing our unique talents, pursuing our passions, and contributing to the well-being of ourselves and others, we can embark on a transformative journey that leads to a deeper understanding of ourselves and a greater connection to the world around us. It is a journey worth undertaking, for it is in the pursuit of self-actualization that we truly discover who we are and what we are capable of becoming. The ascent to self is a continuous climb, a testament to the enduring power of the human spirit to strive, to learn, and to ultimately, self-actualize.

THE CONCEPT
of Self-Actualization

As we previously discussed, self-actualization is a pivotal concept in humanistic psychology, originally popularized by Abraham Maslow in his hierarchy of needs. It represents the culmination of personal development, where an individual realizes their full potential and engages in the pursuit of personal growth and self-improvement. Unlike basic needs such as food and safety, which must be met first, self-actualization emerges when individuals seek deeper meaning and fulfillment in their lives. It drives people to explore their talents, creativity, and aspirations, ultimately leading to a more authentic existence.

The process of self-actualization is unique to each individual and often involves a journey of introspection and self-discovery. Individuals may engage in various activities that challenge their limits, such as pursuing creative endeavors, engaging in meaningful relationships, or seeking new experiences. This exploration not only fosters a sense of purpose but also cultivates resilience and adaptability in the face of life's challenges. As individuals embrace their true selves, they may find greater satisfaction and a sense of belonging in the world around them.

Self-actualization is closely linked to the concept of personal authenticity. To be self-actualized, one must have a clear understanding of their values, beliefs, and desires. This alignment between inner self and outer actions allows individuals to live in accordance with their true nature, leading to a more harmonious existence. Authenticity also encourages individuals to accept their flaws and limitations, which is essential for personal growth. By recognizing and embracing their imperfections, individuals can cultivate a sense of self-compassion and foster a more profound connection with others.

Moreover, self-actualization is not a static state but rather a dynamic process that evolves throughout life. As individuals encounter new experiences and challenges, their understanding of themselves may shift, leading to new aspirations and goals. This ongoing journey encourages a mindset of lifelong learning, where individuals remain open to self-reflection and growth. Engaging with diverse perspectives and experiences can enrich this process, allowing individuals to expand their horizons and continually redefine what it means for them to be self-actualized.

In summary, the concept of self-actualization serves as a guiding principle for individuals seeking to navigate the complexities of human existence. By understanding and embracing this journey, adults can cultivate a deeper connection with themselves and others, ultimately leading to a more fulfilling life. The pursuit of self-actualization encourages individuals to explore their potential, foster authenticity, and engage in lifelong learning, enriching their emotional and existential experiences within the human spectrum.

BARRIERS *to* Self-Actualization

Self-actualization, the process of realizing one's full potential, often encounters numerous barriers that impede individuals on their journey toward personal growth. These barriers can stem from various sources, including societal norms, internal conflicts, and environmental factors. Understanding these obstacles is essential for anyone striving to achieve a higher state of being and fulfillment in life. By identifying and addressing these barriers, individuals can create pathways to self-actualization that are more accessible and achievable.

One of the most significant barriers to self-actualization is the influence of societal expectations and cultural norms. Many individuals find themselves conforming to the roles and standards set by society, which can stifle their individuality and creativity. This pressure to fit into predefined molds can lead to a sense of disconnection from one's true self. For example, the pursuit of success as defined by societal standards—wealth, status, and prestige—often diverts attention away from personal values and authentic desires. This dissonance can create a profound sense of dissatisfaction, making it challenging for individuals to pursue their genuine aspirations.

Internal conflicts also pose substantial challenges to self-actualization. Individuals may grapple with self-doubt, fear of failure, or feelings of unworthiness that can hinder their progress. These internalized beliefs often originate from past experiences, negative feedback, or critical self-talk. The fear of taking risks or stepping outside one's comfort zone can prevent individuals from exploring new opportunities for growth. Recognizing these internal barriers is crucial, as it allows individuals to challenge and reframe these limiting beliefs, paving the way for a more fulfilling life.

Environmental factors, such as socioeconomic status and access to education, can significantly impact an individual's ability to pursue self-actualization. Those who experience financial instability or lack access to resources may find it difficult to focus on personal growth when basic needs are not met. Additionally, a lack of supportive relationships can exacerbate feelings of isolation and hinder self-exploration. Creating an environment that nurtures growth, whether through supportive social networks or access to educational opportunities, can help mitigate these barriers and encourage individuals to realize their potential.

Lastly, the journey toward self-actualization is often complicated by the fast pace of modern life. The demands of work, family, and social obligations can leave little time for self-reflection and inner exploration. Individuals may become so preoccupied with daily responsibilities that they neglect their personal development. To overcome this barrier, it is essential to prioritize self-care and allocate time for introspection. Engaging in practices such as mindfulness, journaling, or therapy can facilitate this process, enabling individuals to reconnect with their inner selves and foster a deeper understanding of their desires and motivations. By recognizing and addressing these barriers, individuals can embark on a more meaningful journey toward self-actualization.

Strategies *for* Achieving Personal Growth

Personal growth is a multifaceted journey that requires intentional effort and a willingness to explore both the inner self and external influences. One effective strategy for achieving personal growth is the practice of self-reflection. By regularly assessing one's thoughts, emotions, and behaviors, individuals can identify patterns that hinder their development. Journaling, meditation, or engaging in mindful practices can facilitate this process. Self-reflection allows individuals to confront their beliefs and values, fostering a deeper understanding of oneself and paving the way for meaningful change.

Another essential strategy is setting specific, measurable, achievable, relevant, and time-bound (SMART) goals. Goals provide direction and motivation, serving as a roadmap for personal development. By breaking larger ambitions into smaller, manageable steps, individuals can track their progress and celebrate small victories along the way. This approach not only enhances focus but also cultivates resilience, as individuals learn to navigate challenges and setbacks while remaining committed to their objectives.

Cultivating a growth mindset is also pivotal in the pursuit of personal growth. This concept, developed by psychologist Carol Dweck, emphasizes the belief that abilities and intelligence can be developed through dedication and hard work. Embracing challenges, persisting through difficulties, and viewing failures as opportunities for learning are hallmarks of a growth mindset. By shifting one's perspective on intelligence and success, individuals can foster a more adaptive approach to personal growth, allowing them to embrace new experiences and continuously evolve.

Engaging in meaningful relationships can significantly enhance personal growth. Humanistic psychology emphasizes the importance of connection and empathy in the development of an individual's potential. Building a supportive network of friends, mentors, or community members can provide encouragement and diverse perspectives that enrich one's journey. These relationships can serve as mirrors, reflecting back insights and helping individuals to confront their blind spots, ultimately leading to deeper self-awareness and growth.

Practicing self-compassion is crucial for sustaining personal growth. Many individuals are their own harshest critics, which can stifle progress and lead to feelings of inadequacy. By treating oneself with kindness and understanding during times of struggle, individuals can create a safe space for exploration and growth. Self-compassion fosters resilience, allowing individuals to face challenges without fear of judgment. This nurturing approach to oneself can transform the journey of personal growth into a more fulfilling and enriching experience.

EMOTIONS IN RELATIONSHIPS
The Role of Emotions *in* Interpersonal Dynamics

Emotions play a pivotal role in shaping interpersonal dynamics, influencing how individuals relate to one another and navigate their social environments. From the simplest interactions to the most complex relationships, emotions serve as both a catalyst for connection and a potential source of conflict. Understanding this dual role can illuminate the intricacies of human behavior and enhance our capacity for empathy and communication. Emotions function as social signals, conveying our internal states and prompting reactions in others, which can lead to both positive and negative outcomes in relationships.

At the center of interpersonal dynamics is the concept of emotional intelligence, which encompasses the ability to recognize, understand, and manage one's own emotions as well as those of others. Individuals with high emotional intelligence are often more adept at navigating social complexities, as they can interpret emotional cues, respond appropriately, and foster meaningful connections. This skill not only enhances personal relationships but also improves professional interactions, highlighting the significance of emotions in various spheres of life. Recognizing the emotional undercurrents in any interaction allows for deeper understanding and better conflict resolution.

Furthermore, emotions are intricately linked to the development of trust and intimacy within relationships. Positive emotions such as joy, love, and gratitude can strengthen bonds and promote a sense of belonging. Conversely, negative emotions such as anger, jealousy, and fear can create barriers and lead to misunderstandings. The interplay of these emotional states influences how individuals perceive one another and affects their willingness to engage authentically. Building trust requires emotional vulnerability, and the willingness to share one's feelings can deepen connections and foster a supportive environment.

The impact of cultural differences on emotional expression and interpretation cannot be overlooked in the context of interpersonal dynamics. Various cultures have distinct norms regarding which emotions are acceptable to express and how they should be conveyed. Misinterpretations can arise when individuals from different cultural backgrounds interact, leading to confusion or conflict. Awareness of these differences is crucial for effective communication and can aid in bridging gaps between diverse emotional landscapes. This understanding fosters respect and appreciation for the rich tapestry of human experience, enhancing interpersonal relations.

The role of emotions in interpersonal dynamics underscores the essence of humanity. Emotions enrich our lives, providing depth to our experiences and shaping our interactions. As we navigate the complexities of our relationships, developing emotional awareness and intelligence becomes essential. By recognizing the power of emotions, we can cultivate healthier connections, promote empathy, and create a more harmonious existence.

Embracing the emotional spectrum not only enhances personal well-being but also contributes to the overall fabric of society, highlighting the interdependence of our emotional lives and our shared humanity.

COMMUNICATING
Emotions Effectively

Communicating emotions effectively is a cornerstone of human interaction and understanding. It involves the ability to express feelings in a manner that is clear and resonates with others. This process allows individuals to share their internal experiences, fostering empathy and connection. In humanistic psychology, the emphasis on authentic communication aligns with the belief that each person possesses inherent worth and the potential for personal growth. By articulating emotions honestly, individuals can create meaningful relationships that enhance their emotional well-being.

One essential aspect of effective emotional communication is self-awareness. Understanding one's own feelings is the precursor to expressing them to others. This self-reflection can involve recognizing the nuances of different emotions, such as distinguishing between anger and frustration or sadness and disappointment. When individuals take the time to reflect on their emotional states, they can better articulate their needs and desires. This clarity not only helps in personal communication but also aids in navigating social interactions, as it reduces the likelihood of misunderstandings.

Active listening plays a crucial role in the exchange of emotions. It involves fully engaging with the speaker, demonstrating empathy, and validating their feelings. This practice fosters an environment where individuals feel safe to express their emotions without fear of judgment. In a world where many feel isolated, active listening can bridge the gap between individuals, allowing them to connect on a deeper level. By being present and attentive, listeners can help articulate feelings that the speaker may struggle to express, enhancing mutual understanding and support.

Non-verbal communication is another critical component in conveying emotions effectively. Body language, facial expressions, and tone of voice can significantly influence how emotions are perceived. For instance, a warm smile or a gentle tone can convey understanding and compassion, while crossed arms or a tense voice may convey defensiveness or discomfort. Being mindful of these non-verbal cues can enhance communication and ensure that the intended emotions are accurately expressed and received. This alignment between verbal and non-verbal communication fosters trust and openness in relationships.

Developing emotional intelligence is vital for effective communication. Emotional intelligence encompasses the ability to recognize, understand, and manage one's own emotions while also empathizing with the emotions of others. Individuals with high emotional intelligence are often better equipped to navigate complex social dynamics and resolve conflicts. By investing in emotional intelligence, adults can enhance their ability to communicate emotions clearly and constructively. This not only benefits personal relationships but also contributes to a more compassionate and understanding society, ultimately enriching the human experience.

Navigating Conflict *through* Emotional Awareness

Navigating conflict effectively requires a deep understanding of emotional awareness, particularly within the realm of humanistic psychology. This approach emphasizes the importance of recognizing and validating one's own feelings as well as those of others. Emotional awareness serves as a foundational element in managing interpersonal disputes, allowing individuals to respond to conflicts with empathy rather than defensiveness. By fostering an environment where emotions are acknowledged, individuals can transform potential confrontations into opportunities for growth and understanding.

Emotional awareness involves the ability to identify and articulate one's feelings in real-time. This skill is crucial during conflicts, as heightened emotions can often cloud judgment and lead to reactive behaviors. Practicing mindfulness can enhance this awareness, enabling individuals to pause and reflect before responding. By taking a moment to assess their emotional state, individuals can better understand their triggers and motivations, which can be instrumental in de-escalating conflicts. This self-awareness not only aids in personal reflection but also paves the way for more meaningful communication with others.

Recognizing the emotional landscape of others is equally important in conflict resolution. Humanistic psychology emphasizes empathy as a means to connect with others on a deeper level. By actively listening and validating the feelings of those involved in the conflict, individuals can create a safe space for open dialogue. This approach fosters mutual respect and understanding, which are essential components of resolving disputes amicably. When individuals feel heard and valued, they are more likely to engage collaboratively rather than adversarial, reducing the likelihood of escalation.

In addition to empathy, cultivating emotional intelligence plays a vital role in navigating conflict. Emotional intelligence encompasses the ability to manage one's own emotions while also being attuned to the emotions of others. This dual focus allows individuals to respond to conflicts with a level of sophistication that can lead to productive outcomes. By employing strategies such as reframing negative thoughts and practicing self-regulation, individuals can maintain composure during heated situations. This not only aids in personal conflict management but also sets a positive example for others involved.

Navigating conflict through emotional awareness is a critical skill that enriches human connections and enhances overall well-being. By embracing this approach, individuals can cultivate healthier relationships and foster environments where open communication thrives. The principles of humanistic psychology underscore the importance of empathy, self-awareness, and emotional intelligence in conflict resolution. As individuals become more adept at recognizing and addressing their own emotions and those of others, they contribute to a more compassionate and understanding society.

THE IMPACT OF SOCIETY ON EMOTIONS

Social Constructs and Emotional Norms

Social constructs and emotional norms play a significant role in shaping human experiences and interactions. These constructs influence how individuals express their feelings, perceive the emotions of others, and engage in social relationships. From early childhood, people learn about acceptable emotional behaviors through cultural narratives and societal expectations. These norms dictate which emotions are deemed appropriate in various contexts, such as workplace environments, family settings, and public spaces. As a result, individuals often navigate a complex landscape of emotional expression that is heavily influenced by the expectations of their social environment.

The concept of emotional norms varies across cultures, reflecting diverse values and beliefs about emotions. In some cultures, open expression of feelings, such as joy or sorrow, is encouraged and celebrated, while others may promote emotional restraint and composure. This divergence can lead to misunderstandings and conflicts in interpersonal relationships, especially in multicultural settings. Adults engaging with individuals from different backgrounds may find themselves challenged to adapt their emotional expressions to align with varying cultural expectations, fostering a deeper understanding of the richness of human emotion.

Moreover, social constructs related to gender also significantly impact emotional norms. Traditional views often dictate that men should exhibit stoicism and strength, while women may be encouraged to express vulnerability and empathy. These gendered expectations can inhibit authentic emotional expression, leading to internal conflict for individuals who feel pressured to conform to societal standards. As adults grapple with these norms, they may experience a range of emotions, from frustration to liberation, as they seek to navigate their own identities and emotional truths.

In recent years, there has been a growing movement towards emotional authenticity and awareness. This shift encourages individuals to challenge traditional emotional norms and embrace a more holistic understanding of their feelings. Humanistic psychology emphasizes the importance of self-actualization and personal growth, advocating for an environment where individuals can express their emotions freely and authentically. By fostering spaces that value emotional honesty, society can promote healthier relationships and enhance overall emotional well-being.

Understanding social constructs and emotional norms is essential for personal development and social cohesion. Adults who reflect on their emotional experiences and the societal influences that shape them can cultivate a greater sense of empathy and connection with others. By engaging in open dialogues about emotions and challenging restrictive norms, individuals can contribute to a more inclusive society that honors the complexity of the human experience, ultimately enriching their own lives and the lives of those around them.

The Influence *of* Media *and* Technology

The influence of media and technology on human emotions and interactions is profound and multifaceted. As we delve into the intricacies of human existence, it becomes increasingly evident that the ways in which we communicate, express, and understand our emotions are shaped significantly by the tools and platforms available to us. Media, in its various forms, serves as both a mirror and a mold for societal values and individual beliefs, reflecting cultural narratives while simultaneously shaping our understanding of the self and others.

The rise of digital media has transformed the landscape of human connection. Social media platforms allow individuals to share experiences, thoughts, and emotions instantaneously, fostering a sense of community that transcends geographical boundaries. However, this hyper-connectivity can lead to superficial interactions and a dilution of genuine emotional engagement. The nature of online communication often lacks the nuances of face-to-face interactions, such as tone of voice and body language, which can lead to misunderstandings and emotional disconnection. As individuals navigate their emotional landscapes, the challenge lies in balancing the benefits of connectivity with the risks of isolation and miscommunication.

Media representations of emotions and relationships significantly impact societal norms and individual self-perception. Television shows, films, and online content often idealize certain emotional experiences while stigmatizing others, creating a framework through which people evaluate their own feelings. This can lead to unrealistic expectations regarding emotional expression and the pursuit of happiness. The portrayal of mental health in media, for instance, can either foster empathy and understanding or perpetuate harmful stereotypes, influencing how individuals relate to their own emotional struggles and those of others.

Technology also plays a crucial role in the evolution of emotional intelligence. With the advent of apps and platforms designed for mental health support, individuals have greater access to resources that promote emotional awareness and regulation. These tools can facilitate self-reflection and provide strategies for managing difficult emotions, thereby enhancing overall well-being. However, reliance on technology for emotional support raises questions about the authenticity of these interactions and the potential for over-reliance on digital solutions at the expense of human connection.

The relationship between media, technology, and human emotions is a complex and evolving dynamic. As we continue to navigate existence in an increasingly digital world, it is essential to remain mindful of how these influences shape our emotional experiences and interpersonal relationships. By fostering an awareness of the effects of media and technology, we can strive for a more balanced approach that honors the depth of human emotion while embracing the opportunities for connection and growth that modern advancements provide.

COPING MECHANISMS AND EMOTIONAL RESILIENCE

Understanding Coping Strategies

Coping strategies are essential tools that individuals develop to manage stress, anxiety, and the various challenges life presents. Understanding these strategies is crucial for fostering emotional resilience and promoting mental well-being. Coping mechanisms can be categorized into two primary types: problem-focused and emotion-focused strategies. Problem-focused strategies involve actively addressing the issue at hand, aiming to reduce or eliminate the source of stress. In contrast, emotion-focused strategies seek to manage the emotional distress associated with the situation, often by reframing thoughts or seeking social support. Recognizing these categories helps individuals identify their own coping preferences and understand how these preferences impact their emotional health.

Effective coping strategies can vary significantly from person to person, influenced by personality, life experiences, and cultural background. For instance, some individuals may find solace in creative expression, such as art or writing, while others might prefer physical activities like exercise or sports to channel their emotions. The diversity in coping mechanisms underscores the importance of self-awareness and personal reflection in navigating one's emotional landscape. By exploring different coping strategies, individuals can tailor their approaches to better suit their unique circumstances and emotional needs.

The effectiveness of a coping strategy often depends on the context in which it is employed. Situational factors, such as the severity of the stressor, available resources, and social support systems, can significantly influence how well a particular strategy works. For example, seeking social support may be an effective emotion-focused strategy during times of loss or grief, as connecting with others can provide comfort and understanding. Conversely, in situations requiring immediate problem-solving, such as work-related stress, a problem-focused approach may yield better results. Understanding the nuances of context is essential for individuals to adapt their coping strategies effectively.

The development of coping strategies can also be a dynamic process. As individuals encounter new experiences and challenges throughout their lives, their coping mechanisms may evolve. Life transitions, such as entering a new job, starting a family, or coping with aging, can prompt individuals to reassess their coping strategies and adopt new ones that better fit their current reality. This adaptability is a vital component of emotional health, as it allows individuals to remain resilient in the face of change.

Continuous learning about oneself and the effectiveness of various strategies can lead to enhanced coping skills over time.

In the realm of humanistic psychology, the emphasis on self-actualization and personal growth aligns closely with the understanding of coping strategies. By fostering a deeper awareness of emotional responses and the strategies employed to manage them, individuals can cultivate a more profound connection with their authentic selves. This journey not only aids in coping with immediate challenges but also contributes to a broader understanding of the human experience. Embracing the diversity of coping strategies allows individuals to celebrate their humanity, acknowledging that while struggles are universal, the paths to navigate them are uniquely personal.

Building Emotional Resilience

Building emotional resilience is essential for navigating the complexities of life, particularly in an era marked by rapid change and uncertainty. Emotional resilience refers to the capacity to adapt and bounce back from adversity, stress, and challenges. It is a dynamic process that involves both the internal resources of the individual and the external support systems available to them. Understanding and cultivating emotional resilience can lead to improved mental well-being, a deeper sense of purpose, and stronger interpersonal relationships.

One of the foundational aspects of building emotional resilience is self-awareness. Individuals must first recognize their emotional responses and triggers to develop effective coping strategies. Self-awareness involves identifying feelings, understanding the underlying causes, and acknowledging how these emotions influence behavior. Techniques such as mindfulness and reflective journaling can aid in this process, allowing individuals to cultivate a deeper understanding of their emotional landscape. By enhancing self-awareness, individuals can create a solid foundation upon which they can build their resilience.

Another crucial element is the development of a positive mindset. Adopting a perspective that views challenges as opportunities for growth rather than insurmountable obstacles can significantly enhance emotional resilience. This shift in thinking encourages individuals to embrace change and uncertainty with curiosity and openness. Cognitive-behavioral techniques, such as reframing negative thoughts and practicing gratitude, can help individuals foster a more optimistic outlook. When individuals learn to frame their experiences positively, they are better equipped to face difficulties and maintain their emotional balance.

Building strong, supportive relationships is also vital in enhancing emotional resilience. Social connections provide a critical source of support during times of stress and hardship. Engaging in meaningful interactions with friends, family, and community members can create a safety net that fosters resilience. These relationships not only offer emotional support but also provide diverse perspectives and resources that can help individuals navigate their challenges.

Cultivating a sense of belonging and community can significantly bolster one's ability to cope with adversity.

The practice of self-care cannot be overlooked in the quest for emotional resilience. Prioritizing physical health, engaging in activities that bring joy, and ensuring adequate rest are essential components of self-care. This holistic approach to well-being allows individuals to recharge and maintain their emotional equilibrium. Mindful practices, such as yoga, meditation, and physical exercise, can also enhance emotional regulation and provide tools for managing stress. Ultimately, building emotional resilience is a multifaceted endeavor that requires a commitment to self-awareness, positive thinking, supportive relationships, and self-care, all of which contribute to a more fulfilling and balanced life.

The Importance *of* Mindfulness *and* Self-Care

Mindfulness and self-care are essential practices that significantly enhance our emotional well-being and overall quality of life. In an age marked by relentless demands and constant distractions, cultivating mindfulness allows individuals to ground themselves in the present moment. This practice encourages a heightened awareness of thoughts, feelings, and bodily sensations, fostering a deeper understanding of one's internal landscape. By engaging fully with the present, individuals can better navigate the complexities of their emotions, leading to improved mental health and resilience.

Self-care complements mindfulness by emphasizing the importance of nurturing oneself both physically and emotionally. It encompasses a range of activities and practices that promote well-being, such as maintaining a balanced diet, exercising, and engaging in hobbies. More than mere indulgence, self-care is a vital component of a healthy lifestyle that acknowledges one's needs and responds to them with compassion. This proactive approach not only alleviates stress but also cultivates a sense of self-worth and empowerment, fostering a positive relationship with oneself.

In the context of humanistic psychology, mindfulness and self-care are integral to the pursuit of personal growth and self-actualization. Humanistic psychology emphasizes the inherent worth of individuals and their potential for fulfillment. By integrating mindfulness into daily routines, individuals can explore their values, desires, and aspirations, leading to a more authentic existence. This self-exploration, coupled with self-care practices, encourages a holistic approach to personal development, where emotional, mental, and physical health are interconnected.

Moreover, the societal implications of mindfulness and self-care cannot be overlooked. In a world where stress and anxiety are prevalent, fostering a culture that prioritizes these practices can lead to healthier communities. When individuals engage in mindfulness, they are more likely to approach challenges with empathy and understanding, promoting harmonious relationships and social cohesion. By normalizing self-care, society can reduce stigma around mental health issues, encouraging individuals to seek help and support when needed.

The importance of mindfulness and self-care extends beyond individual benefits; they are vital for cultivating a compassionate and resilient society. By embracing these practices, individuals can enhance their emotional intelligence, improve their relationships, and contribute positively to their communities. As we navigate the complexities of existence, mindfulness and self-care serve as essential tools for fostering a deeper connection to ourselves and others, enriching the human experience in profound ways.

THE FUTURE OF HUMAN EMOTIONS
Evolution *of* Emotional Understanding

The evolution of emotional understanding is a profound journey that spans centuries, reflecting the intricate relationship between human development and the shifting paradigms of psychology. Early philosophical inquiry into emotions can be traced back to thinkers like Aristotle, who viewed emotions as vital components of human experience, shaping moral judgments and ethical behavior. This foundational perspective laid the groundwork for later psychological theories, which began to categorize and analyze emotions more systematically. As the field of psychology emerged in the late 19th century, scholars began to explore the complexity of emotions, leading to a greater appreciation for their role in the human experience.

With the advent of psychoanalysis in the early 20th century, Sigmund Freud introduced the idea that unconscious emotions significantly influence behavior and interpersonal relationships. His theories emphasized the importance of understanding one's inner emotional world to achieve psychological well-being. This focus on the unconscious opened new avenues for exploring emotional depth, paving the way for subsequent psychological movements that sought to unravel the intricacies of human feelings. During this era, the recognition of emotions as both conscious and unconscious processes became a cornerstone of psychological inquiry, further enriching our understanding of emotional dynamics.

As humanistic psychology emerged in the mid-20th century, figures like Carl Rogers and Abraham Maslow shifted the focus toward the individual's subjective emotional experiences. They championed the idea that self-actualization and personal growth are intrinsically linked to emotional awareness and acceptance. This perspective emphasized the inherent value of emotions in fostering authentic connections with oneself and others. Humanistic psychology underscored the importance of empathy and compassion, advocating for a holistic understanding of individuals that incorporates emotional, social, and psychological dimensions. This shift marked a significant evolution in emotional understanding, moving away from purely mechanistic views of human behavior.

In recent decades, advances in neuroscience and psychology have further illuminated the complexities of emotional understanding. Research on emotional intelligence, pioneered by Daniel Goleman, has highlighted the significance of recognizing, understanding, and managing emotions in oneself and others. This has led to a broader recognition of emotions as a fundamental component of effective communication, decision-making, and overall well-being. The integration of emotional intelligence into educational and professional settings has transformed how individuals navigate their emotions, fostering environments that prioritize emotional literacy and resilience.

The evolution of emotional understanding continues to unfold as society grapples with the challenges of modern life. Increasing awareness of mental health issues and the role of emotions in psychological disorders has prompted a reevaluation of how emotions are perceived and addressed in therapeutic settings. Contemporary approaches to mental health emphasize the importance of emotional regulation and the cultivation of emotional skills, reflecting a growing recognition of the integral role emotions play in the human experience. As we advance in our understanding of emotions, it becomes clear that emotional awareness is not just a personal journey but a collective endeavor that shapes our interactions, relationships, and ultimately, the essence of humanity itself.

The Role *of* Psychology *in* Modern Society

Psychology plays a crucial role in modern society by providing insights into human behavior, thoughts, and emotions. As individuals navigate the complexities of daily life, understanding psychological principles can enhance personal well-being and interpersonal relationships. The evolution of psychology has led to a greater emphasis on humanistic approaches, which prioritize individual experience and personal growth. This shift has allowed for a more nuanced understanding of what it means to be human, fostering a society that values empathy, compassion, and self-actualization.

Humanistic psychology, with its focus on the inherent goodness of people and their potential for growth, serves as a foundational element in contemporary psychological practices. This approach emphasizes the importance of personal agency and the subjective experience of individuals. Therapists who adopt humanistic principles often create safe and supportive environments that encourage clients to explore their feelings and aspirations. By prioritizing the individual's unique perspective, humanistic psychology contributes to a deeper understanding of human motivations and the factors that influence behavior.

In addition to therapeutic settings, the principles of psychology are increasingly applied in educational contexts and corporate environments. Educators utilize psychological theories to create engaging and effective learning experiences, recognizing that students are not merely vessels for information but individuals with diverse emotional and cognitive needs. Similarly, organizations are recognizing the importance of employee well-being and team dynamics, integrating psychological insights into their management practices. This holistic approach not only improves productivity but also fosters a workplace culture that honors the emotional and psychological well-being of its members.

The role of psychology extends beyond individual and organizational frameworks; it also shapes public policy and community initiatives. Understanding the psychological underpinnings of social issues, such as mental health, addiction, and violence, allows policymakers to develop more effective interventions. By incorporating psychological research into social planning, communities can create programs that address the root causes of problems rather than merely treating symptoms. This approach promotes a healthier society by fostering resilience, reducing stigma, and encouraging support systems that empower individuals.

As society continues to evolve, the importance of psychology in understanding and addressing human behavior cannot be overstated. The insights gained from psychological research inform various fields, from mental health care to education and social justice. By embracing humanistic psychology and its emphasis on the essence of humanity, individuals and communities can cultivate a deeper appreciation for emotional experiences and foster environments conducive to growth and healing. Ultimately, psychology serves as a vital tool in navigating the complexities of existence, helping people lead more fulfilling and connected lives.

Embracing Emotional Diversity *in the* Future

Embracing emotional diversity in the future is a crucial step toward understanding the full spectrum of human experience. As society evolves, so too does the recognition of varied emotional expressions and the importance of acknowledging these differences. Emotional diversity encompasses a wide range of feelings, expressions, and responses, all influenced by cultural, social, and individual factors. An awareness of this diversity can foster deeper connections among individuals, enhance empathy, and contribute to a more inclusive society that celebrates rather than suppresses emotional expression.

In the realm of humanistic psychology, which emphasizes personal growth and self-actualization, the acceptance of emotional diversity becomes a foundational principle. Humanistic psychologists advocate for the recognition of each individual's unique emotional landscape as a vital aspect of their humanity. This perspective allows for a more holistic approach to mental health, where emotional differences are not seen as deficits but rather as rich tapestries of human experience. By promoting an environment where diverse emotions are validated, we can encourage individuals to explore and express their feelings more freely.

The future of emotional diversity will likely be shaped by advancements in technology and communication. As digital platforms become integral to human interaction, they offer new ways to express and share emotions. Online communities provide spaces where individuals can connect over shared emotional experiences, breaking down geographical and cultural barriers. However, this also presents challenges, as the digital realm can sometimes dilute or misrepresent genuine emotional expression. It is essential to navigate this landscape carefully, ensuring that emotional diversity is celebrated rather than commodified or trivialized.

Education will play a vital role in fostering emotional diversity in future generations. By integrating emotional intelligence and diversity training into educational curricula, we can equip individuals with the tools to understand and appreciate different emotional expressions from an early age. Schools and institutions must encourage open discussions about feelings and provide safe spaces for students to explore their emotional identities. This proactive approach not only enhances individual well-being but also cultivates empathy and compassion among peers, laying the groundwork for a more emotionally aware society.

Embracing emotional diversity is an ongoing journey that requires commitment and openness from individuals and communities alike. As we move forward, it is essential to create platforms for dialogue and understanding, allowing for the sharing of diverse emotional narratives. By prioritizing emotional diversity, we honor the essence of humanity—acknowledging that our emotional experiences, both unique and collective, are what bind us together. In doing so, we pave the way for a future characterized by greater understanding, acceptance, and celebration of the rich emotional tapestry that defines human existence.

To build a culture of emotional intelligence is to recognize that the true measure of our humanity lies not in our intellectual prowess, but in our capacity to feel, to understand, and to respond with compassion to the emotional currents that flow through ourselves and through the world around us.

HUMANISM IN ACTION PSYCHOLOGY S ROLE IN SOCIAL JUSTICE MOVEMENTS

Introduction to Humanism *and* Social Justice

Defining Humanism

Humanism is a philosophical and ethical stance that emphasizes the value and agency of human beings, individually and collectively. At its core, humanism advocates for a focus on human needs and concerns, prioritizing human dignity, welfare, and the potential for personal and collective growth. It seeks to understand the human experience through reason, empathy, and compassion, often placing a strong emphasis on the importance of emotional intelligence. This emotional awareness is crucial not only in personal development but also in leadership, therapy, and community engagement, serving as a foundation for fostering meaningful connections and understanding among individuals.

In the realm of mental health therapy, humanistic approaches prioritize the individual's capacity for self-actualization and personal growth. Therapists who adopt a humanistic framework often utilize techniques that promote self-discovery and emotional awareness, allowing clients to explore their feelings and experiences in a supportive environment. This approach recognizes the inherent worth of each person, facilitating a therapeutic alliance built on trust and empathy. By integrating emotional intelligence into therapy, practitioners can better guide clients in navigating their emotional landscapes, ultimately leading to improved mental health outcomes and a deeper understanding of the self.

Understanding humanism is also crucial in the context of leadership development, where emotional intelligence plays a pivotal role. Effective leaders are those who not only possess cognitive skills but also demonstrate empathy, self-awareness, and social awareness. These emotional competencies enable leaders to connect with their teams on a deeper level, fostering an inclusive and supportive workplace culture. By embracing humanistic principles, leaders can redefine success, moving beyond traditional metrics of productivity to prioritize the well-being of their employees and the common good. This shift promotes a healthier organizational environment and enhances overall job satisfaction and engagement.

In addressing social justice movements, humanism serves as a guiding principle that emphasizes the importance of collective action for the common good. Humanistic psychology advocates for social change that uplifts marginalized communities, recognizing the interconnectedness of all individuals. By integrating emotional intelligence into advocacy efforts, activists can communicate more effectively and empathetically, bridging divides and fostering understanding among diverse groups. This approach not only strengthens community bonds but also empowers individuals to contribute meaningfully to societal change, reinforcing the idea that social justice is a shared responsibility that benefits everyone.

Humanism's emphasis on community building through enhanced social values highlights the importance of collaboration and mutual respect in fostering societal well-being. Emotional intelligence is essential in nurturing these values, as it enables individuals to engage with one another thoughtfully and compassionately. By cultivating emotional skills in parenting, workplace dynamics, and community interactions, individuals can create environments where empathy and understanding flourish. This transformation ultimately contributes to a redefinition of success—one that prioritizes well-being, social equity, and the common good, aligning with the core tenets of humanism.

The Intersection of Psychology *and* Social Justice

The intersection of psychology and social justice represents a crucial area of exploration that highlights the profound impact of mental health and emotional intelligence on societal structures. At this crossroads, humanistic psychology emerges as a guiding framework that emphasizes the inherent worth of individuals and the importance of fostering environments conducive to personal growth and social equity. By prioritizing empathy, compassion, and understanding, psychological principles can inform social justice initiatives, creating pathways for more inclusive and equitable communities.

Emotional intelligence plays a pivotal role in leadership development, particularly in the context of social justice. Leaders equipped with high emotional intelligence are better positioned to understand and navigate the complexities of diverse social issues. They can foster collaborative environments that encourage open dialogue, actively listen to marginalized voices, and facilitate conflict resolution. Moreover, such leaders are more adept at recognizing their biases and understanding the emotional undercurrents that influence group dynamics, thereby enhancing their capacity to enact meaningful change.

In therapeutic settings, humanistic approaches to mental health therapy underscore the importance of individual agency and the social context in which people operate. Therapists who integrate social justice principles into their practice not only address personal struggles but also recognize the systemic barriers that affect mental health outcomes. This dual focus fosters a more holistic understanding of well-being, emphasizing the interplay between personal experiences and broader societal factors. Such an approach empowers clients to advocate for themselves and their communities, reinforcing the idea that mental health is intricately linked to social equity.

The role of emotional intelligence in conflict resolution further illustrates the intersection of psychology and social justice. By cultivating skills such as empathy and active listening, individuals can engage in more constructive dialogues, reducing tensions and fostering understanding among conflicting parties. This is particularly relevant in community settings where diverse perspectives may clash. Effective conflict resolution rooted in emotional intelligence not only mitigates immediate disputes but also contributes to a culture of respect and collaboration, ultimately enhancing community cohesion and promoting social justice.

Integrating emotional intelligence into parenting techniques is another significant aspect of this intersection. Parents who model emotional awareness and empathetic communication create a nurturing environment that teaches children the values of compassion and social responsibility. This foundational skill set prepares future generations to engage with social justice issues thoughtfully and responsibly. By instilling these principles at an early age, families can contribute to a larger cultural shift that prioritizes well-being and common good principles, ultimately redefining success in terms of collective flourishing rather than individual achievement.

The journey towards a culture of emotional intelligence begins with the courageous act of self-reflection, a willingness to explore the hidden chambers of our own emotional architecture, to acknowledge the shadows and celebrate the light within, and to understand that our own healing is inextricably linked to the healing of the world around us.

WHAT IS EMOTIONAL INTELLIGENCE BEYOND IQ

Beyond the realm of numbers and logic lies a different kind of intelligence, a faculty that dictates how we navigate the complex tapestry of human experience: emotional intelligence. While traditional IQ measures cognitive abilities such as problem-solving and reasoning, emotional intelligence, often referred to as EQ, focuses on our ability to understand, manage, and utilize emotions, both in ourselves and in others. This chapter delves into the core principles of emotional intelligence, highlighting its significance and differentiating it from the more traditionally valued IQ, demonstrating why EQ is increasingly recognized as a critical determinant of success and well-being in both personal and professional spheres.

For decades, IQ was the gold standard for measuring intelligence, dictating academic achievements, career paths, and even perceived life potential. A high IQ was seen as the key to unlocking success, implying an innate superiority in cognitive processing. However, the limitations of relying solely on IQ became increasingly apparent. Brilliant individuals with exceptional academic credentials often found themselves struggling in social situations, unable to connect with others, navigate conflict, or manage their own emotional responses. This led to the realization that something crucial was missing — an understanding of the human element that transcends pure intellect.

Enter emotional intelligence. This multifaceted concept, popularized by Daniel Goleman's groundbreaking work, encompasses five key components: self-awareness, self-regulation, motivation, empathy, and social skills. Self-awareness, the cornerstone of EQ, is the ability to recognize and understand your own emotions, strengths, and weaknesses. It involves tuning into your internal state, understanding how your emotions influence your behavior, and accurately assessing your own capabilities. Without self-awareness, individuals remain vulnerable to emotional hijacking, reacting impulsively and making poor decisions based on fleeting feelings.

Building upon self-awareness is self-regulation, the ability to control and manage your emotions appropriately. This doesn't mean suppressing or denying emotions, but rather understanding how to channel them effectively. Self-regulation allows individuals to remain composed under pressure, manage stress, and adapt to changing circumstances. It fosters resilience, enabling individuals to bounce back from setbacks and maintain a positive outlook even in the face of adversity.

Motivation, driven by an intrinsic desire to achieve goals and persevere through challenges, is another critical component of EQ. Emotionally intelligent individuals are driven by more than just external rewards like money or recognition. They possess a deep-seated passion for their pursuits, a strong sense of purpose, and an unwavering commitment to achieving their objectives. This internal drive fuels their resilience and allows them to overcome obstacles that might deter others.

Empathy, the ability to understand and share the feelings of others, is arguably the most essential component of social intelligence. It involves actively listening, recognizing nonverbal cues, and understanding the perspectives of those around you. Empathy allows individuals to build rapport with others, foster trust, and create strong relationships. It is crucial for effective communication, teamwork, and leadership.

Finally, social skills encompass the ability to manage relationships effectively, communicate persuasively, and navigate social situations with grace and tact. This includes skills such as active listening, conflict resolution, and leadership. Emotionally intelligent individuals are able to build and maintain strong relationships, inspire others, and create a positive and productive environment.

In conclusion, emotional intelligence transcends the limitations of traditional IQ by acknowledging the crucial role of emotions in human behavior and interaction. It is not simply about "feeling good," but about understanding and utilizing the power of emotions to enhance our decision-making, build meaningful relationships, and achieve our goals. As we move further into the 21st century, where collaboration, empathy, and adaptability are increasingly valued, emotional intelligence is no longer a "soft skill," but a critical competency that empowers individuals to thrive in a complex and interconnected world. Embracing and developing our emotional intelligence is investing in a future where human connection and emotional understanding pave the way for greater success and well-being for ourselves and those around us.

THE IMPORTANCE
of Emotional Intelligence

Emotional intelligence (EI) plays a crucial role in various facets of human interaction and development, particularly in leadership, therapy, conflict resolution, and community building. In the context of leadership development, emotional intelligence equips leaders with the ability to understand and manage their own emotions while also empathizing with the feelings of others. This dual capability fosters an environment of trust and open communication, which is essential for effective team dynamics. Leaders who demonstrate high emotional intelligence are better prepared to motivate their teams and navigate the complexities of interpersonal relationships, ultimately leading to enhanced organizational performance.

In the realm of mental health therapy, humanistic approaches emphasize the importance of emotional intelligence in cultivating therapeutic relationships. Therapists who exhibit strong emotional intelligence can better connect with their clients, creating a safe space for self-exploration and healing. By recognizing and validating clients' emotions, therapists not only facilitate deeper understanding but also empower individuals to develop their own emotional awareness and regulation skills. This process is vital for fostering resilience and promoting overall mental well-being, which aligns with the principles of humanistic psychology.

Conflict resolution is another area where emotional intelligence proves essential. The ability to perceive, evaluate, and respond to emotions—both one's own and those of others—enables individuals to navigate disputes with greater effectiveness. Emotional intelligence allows for a more compassionate approach to conflict, encouraging collaboration rather than confrontation. By integrating EI into conflict resolution strategies, individuals can engage in productive dialogues that prioritize understanding and compromise, thereby contributing to more harmonious relationships in both personal and professional settings.

In business ethics, wisdom-based decision-making is increasingly recognized as a key element of sustainable practices. Leaders who incorporate emotional intelligence into their decision-making processes are more likely to consider the broader impact of their choices on stakeholders and the community. This perspective shifts the focus from a mere profit generation to a more holistic view of success that includes well-being and social responsibility. By fostering a culture of emotional intelligence, organizations can cultivate ethical leaders who prioritize the common good and align their business practices with humanistic values.

The integration of emotional intelligence into parenting techniques contributes to the development of emotionally healthy future generations. Parents who practice emotional intelligence are better equipped to model empathy, active listening, and emotional regulation for their children. This nurturing environment fosters strong family bonds and encourages children to develop their own emotional skills. As these children grow into adults, they carry forward the emotional intelligence learned in their formative years, contributing positively to workplace culture, community engagement, and social justice initiatives. Ultimately, emotional intelligence serves as a foundational element in redefining success through well-being and shared human values.

The Anatomy of an Emotion *from* Trigger to Response

Emotions, the vibrant tapestry woven into the fabric of our existence, are often perceived as spontaneous eruptions of feeling. However, beneath the surface of these seemingly sudden surges lies a complex and fascinating anatomy – a carefully orchestrated process that unfolds from the initial trigger to the ultimate expression. Understanding this anatomy, tracing the path from spark to reaction, is not merely an academic exercise; it is the cornerstone of emotional intelligence, enabling us to navigate the world with greater self-awareness and control.

The genesis of any emotion lies in its trigger. These triggers can be broadly categorized into two realms: internal and external. External triggers are readily apparent – a harsh word from a colleague, a sudden setback, a news report detailing a tragedy. These are events, social interactions, and sensory experiences that impinge upon our consciousness and initiate the emotional cascade. Internal triggers, however, are more subtle and often more powerful. These are born from within: memories that resurface unexpectedly, thoughts that spiral into worry, beliefs that shape our perception of the world. A past trauma, for example, can be triggered by a seemingly innocuous smell, instantly transporting us back to a moment of fear and distress. Recognizing both types of triggers is crucial, as it allows us to anticipate potential emotional responses and prepare accordingly.

Once a trigger is activated, a complex interplay of physiological sensations begins to manifest. These physical sensations, often overlooked, are the silent language of our emotions, providing vital clues to the underlying feeling. Anxiety might present as a racing heart, sweaty palms, and a constricted throat. Sadness can manifest as a tightness in the chest, a heavy feeling in the limbs, and a loss of appetite. Anger often results in a flushed face, clenched fists, and a surge of adrenaline. Learning to identify these physical cues is paramount. By paying attention to our bodies, we can become more attuned to our emotional state, recognizing the early warning signs before an emotion escalates into a full-blown crisis. Ignoring these signs is akin to ignoring a warning light on a car dashboard, potentially leading to a more significant breakdown later on.

The final stage in the anatomy of an emotion is the outward expression, the observable behavior that results from the internal process. This is where the critical distinction between reacting and responding comes into play. Reacting is an automatic, often impulsive response driven by the raw power of the emotion itself. It is the uncontrolled outburst of anger, the knee-jerk defense mechanism triggered by fear, the impulsive decision made in the throes of grief. Reacting is often characterized by a lack of conscious thought and can lead to regrettable consequences.

Responding, on the other hand, is a more thoughtful and deliberate action informed by awareness and understanding. It is the result of recognizing the trigger, acknowledging the physical sensations, and consciously choosing a course of action that aligns with our values and goals.

Responding requires a pause, a moment of reflection, a conscious effort to interrupt the automatic cycle of emotion. This pause allows us to assess the situation, consider the potential consequences of our actions, and ultimately choose a response that is both effective and appropriate.

The anatomy of an emotion is a complex yet understandable process. From the initial spark of a trigger, whether internal or external, to the physical sensations that accompany it, and finally to the outward expression, understanding each stage allows us to cultivate emotional intelligence. By learning to identify our triggers, recognize the physical cues of our emotions, and consciously choose to respond rather than react, we can transform our relationship with our emotions, moving from being at their mercy to becoming masters of our own emotional landscape. This mastery is not about suppressing or denying our feelings, but rather about understanding them, accepting them, and using them to navigate the world with greater awareness, empathy, and ultimately, wisdom.

DECODING NON-VERBAL COMMUNICATION
The Silent Language *of* Emotions

Words form the visible tip of the iceberg in the vast ocean of human communication. While we meticulously craft our verbal narratives, a parallel and often more revealing conversation unfolds through the silent language of non-verbal cues. Facial expressions, body language, tone of voice, and the use of personal space – these are the subtle signals that transmit emotions, intentions, and underlying truths, often bypassing our conscious awareness. Mastering the art of decoding this silent language is essential not just for effective communication, but also for fostering genuine understanding and building stronger relationships.

One of the most potent avenues for emotional expression lies in the intricate topography of the human face. While we might consciously project an image of calm and composure, genuine emotions often betray themselves through fleeting micro-expressions. These subtle, involuntary facial movements, lasting only fractions of a second, can reveal concealed joy, anger, fear, or sadness. Recognizing these fleeting glimpses into another person's internal state requires keen observation and practice. A slight tightening of the lips might suggest suppressed anger, while a brief furrowing of the brow could indicate confusion or concern. By honing our ability to decipher these nuanced signals, we gain a deeper understanding of the unspoken emotions driving a conversation.

Beyond the face, the body itself becomes a canvas upon which our emotions are unconsciously painted. Body language, encompassing posture, gestures, and movements, offers a wealth of information about a person's state of mind. A closed-off posture, with arms crossed and shoulders hunched, may signal defensiveness or discomfort. Conversely, an open stance, with relaxed shoulders and uncrossed arms, often indicates openness and receptivity. Similarly, gestures can be incredibly revealing. Fidgeting hands might denote nervousness, while direct eye contact usually implies confidence and sincerity. By carefully observing these non-verbal cues, we can gain valuable insights into a person's feelings and attitudes, even when their words suggest otherwise.

The vocal landscape, too, is rich with emotional undertones. Tone of voice, encompassing pitch, volume, and speed, transforms the meaning of words, adding layers of complexity and often revealing hidden emotions.

Sarcasm, for instance, relies heavily on the use of tone to convey a meaning directly opposite to the literal words spoken. Enthusiasm is often conveyed through an animated and upbeat tone, while hesitation might be signaled by a wavering voice and frequent pauses. Recognizing these vocal cues is crucial for accurately interpreting the speaker's intended message and understanding the emotional context of the conversation. A carefully chosen phrase delivered with a sarcastic tone can have a vastly different impact than the same phrase spoken with sincerity.

Finally, the often-overlooked realm of proxemics, the study of personal space, plays a significant role in non-verbal communication. The distance we maintain from others reflects the nature of our relationship and the level of comfort we feel in their presence. Invading someone's personal space can be perceived as aggressive or intrusive, while maintaining a comfortable distance signals respect and consideration. Intimate relationships are often characterized by close proximity, while professional interactions typically occur at a greater distance. Understanding the unspoken rules of personal space allows us to navigate social situations with greater awareness and avoid inadvertently causing discomfort or misinterpretation.

Decoding non-verbal communication is a vital skill for anyone seeking to improve their understanding of human interaction.

By paying close attention to facial expressions, body language, tone of voice, and the use of personal space, we can unlock a wealth of information about the emotions, intentions, and underlying truths of those around us. This silent language, though often subtle and unconscious, provides invaluable insights into the human experience, enabling us to build stronger relationships, navigate social situations with greater ease, and ultimately, connect with others on a deeper and more meaningful level. Mastering the art of decoding non-verbal cues empowers us to become more empathetic, understanding, and effective communicators, transforming the way we interact with the world.

SELF-REGULATION
Taming *the* Emotional Beast

Once you're aware of your emotions, the next step is learning to manage them effectively. Self-regulation isn't about suppressing your feelings; it's about controlling your reactions and choosing how you respond in different situations.

We'll explore various self-regulation techniques:

1.**COGNITIVE RESTRUCTURING**: Challenging negative or irrational thoughts and replacing them with more balanced perspectives.

We are all, at times, beasts of burden, laden with the weight of our emotions. Joy, sorrow, anger, fear – these powerful forces surge through us, shaping our perceptions, influencing our actions, and ultimately defining the human experience. However, unchecked, these emotional beasts can lead us astray, causing impulsive decisions, strained relationships, and profound personal distress. This is where self-regulation comes into play, acting as the reins that guide our emotional steeds. And among the many tools in the self-regulation arsenal, cognitive restructuring stands out as a particularly effective method, allowing us to tame the emotional beast by challenging negative or irrational thoughts and replacing them with more balanced perspectives.

Cognitive restructuring, at its core, is about changing the way we think. It acknowledges that our feelings are often a direct consequence of our thoughts, not simply a reaction to external events. A minor inconvenience, for instance, can trigger an avalanche of anger if interpreted through a lens of victimization ("Why does this always happen to me?"). Conversely, the same inconvenience might be met with equanimity if viewed as a temporary setback ("It's frustrating, but I can handle it"). This understanding is the foundation upon which cognitive restructuring is built.

The process typically begins with identifying the specific situations that trigger negative emotions. This requires self-awareness and a commitment to observing our own thoughts and feelings. Once a triggering situation is identified, the next step is to pinpoint the automatic negative thoughts (ANTs) that arise in response. These ANTs are often quick, habitual, and seemingly undeniable, like pre-programmed responses to specific stimuli. They might involve catastrophizing ("This is going to ruin everything!"), overgeneralizing ("I always mess things up!"), or personalizing ("It's all my fault!").

However, these "undeniable" thoughts are rarely based on objective reality. This is where the restructuring begins. We must challenge these ANTs by asking ourselves critical questions: What evidence supports this thought? What evidence contradicts it? What are alternative explanations for the situation? Am I exaggerating the consequences? Am I making assumptions without proof? By applying this rigorous scrutiny, we can often uncover the irrationality or exaggeration inherent in our negative thoughts.

The final, and perhaps most crucial, step is to replace these negative thoughts with more balanced and realistic perspectives. This doesn't mean forcing ourselves to think positively in a

Pollyanna-ish fashion. Instead, it involves developing alternative thoughts that are grounded in logic and evidence, acknowledging the complexities of the situation without succumbing to negativity. For example, instead of thinking "I always mess things up," one might replace it with "I made a mistake, but everyone does. I can learn from it and do better next time."

The benefits of cognitive restructuring are manifold. By challenging negative thoughts, we reduce the intensity of negative emotions, allowing us to react to situations with greater clarity and control. This, in turn, improves our ability to make rational decisions, communicate effectively, and maintain healthy relationships. Moreover, with repeated practice, cognitive restructuring can become a habit, altering our default thinking patterns and fostering greater resilience in the face of adversity.

However, cognitive restructuring is not a magic bullet. It requires effort, persistence, and often the guidance of a trained therapist. It can be challenging to identify and challenge our own deeply ingrained negative thinking patterns. Furthermore, it's important to acknowledge that some negative emotions are valid and necessary responses to difficult situations. Cognitive restructuring is not about suppressing emotions; it's about ensuring that our emotional responses are proportional to the reality of the situation and do not contribute to unnecessary suffering.

Self-regulation is the ongoing process of managing our emotions and behaviors in a constructive way. Cognitive restructuring, as a key tool within that process, provides a powerful method for taming the emotional beast. By challenging negative and irrational thoughts and replacing them with more balanced perspectives, we gain greater control over our emotional responses, improve our decision-making abilities, and ultimately lead more fulfilling and resilient lives. It's a journey of self-discovery and mental discipline, but the rewards – a calmer, more rational, and ultimately more empowered self – are well worth the effort.

2. **DEEP BREATHING EXERCISES**: Using controlled breathing to calm your nervous system and reduce stress.

3. **DISTRACTION TECHNIQUES**: Shifting your attention away from triggering situations to regain composure.

4. **SETTING BOUNDARIES**: Protecting your emotional well-being by establishing clear limits on what you're willing to tolerate.

In the tempestuous sea of life, where emotional tides rise and fall without warning, self-regulation acts as our anchor, our rudder, and our very lifeline. It is the ability to manage our emotions, impulses, and behaviors in a healthy and productive manner, allowing us to navigate challenges with grace and achieve our goals with clarity. When self-regulation falters, we become slaves to our emotions, lashing out in anger, succumbing to anxiety, or withdrawing in despair. Mastering this vital skill is not about suppressing emotions, but about understanding them, processing them, and ultimately, taming the emotional beast within. This essay will explore three key strategies for enhancing self-regulation: deep breathing exercises, distraction techniques, and setting boundaries, each acting as a distinct tool in our emotional toolbox.

Deep breathing exercises, the simplest yet profoundly effective technique, work by directly influencing our nervous system. When confronted with a stressful or triggering situation, our bodies often react with the "fight or flight" response. This cascade of physiological changes, including rapid heart rate, shallow breathing, and muscle tension, amplifies feelings of anxiety and panic. Deep breathing, however, acts as an antidote. By consciously slowing down our breathing, taking deep, diaphragmatic breaths, we activate the parasympathetic nervous system, often referred to as the "rest and digest" system. This activation signals to our bodies that we are safe, prompting a cascade of calming hormones that counteract the stress response. The heart rate slows, muscles relax, and the mind begins to clear. In essence, deep breathing provides a momentary pause button, allowing us to regain control before impulsive reactions take over. It's a readily accessible tool, always within reach, providing a grounding force in moments of emotional turmoil.

While deep breathing addresses the physiological aspect of emotional regulation, distraction techniques focus on the psychological. When overwhelmed by negative emotions, our minds tend to ruminate, endlessly circling around the triggering event or thought. This relentless focus intensifies the emotional distress, making it even harder to think clearly and act rationally.

Distraction techniques, in their diverse forms, offer an escape route from this mental loop. Engaging in activities that require our full attention, such as reading a book, listening to music, or practicing a hobby, can effectively shift our focus away from the triggering situation. Physical activity, like going for a walk or engaging in a sport, not only distracts us but also releases endorphins, which have mood-boosting effects. The key lies in choosing activities that are engaging and enjoyable, drawing us away from the negative spiral and allowing us to regain composure. Distraction is not about avoidance; it's about creating a space for objectivity, allowing us to return to the situation with a calmer, more rational perspective.

However, even the most effective breathing exercises and distraction techniques can be rendered futile if we consistently find ourselves in emotionally draining situations. This is where the importance of setting boundaries comes into play.

Boundaries are the invisible lines we draw around ourselves, defining what we are willing to tolerate in our relationships, our work, and our lives in general. They are essential for protecting our emotional well-being and preventing us from being constantly overwhelmed by the needs and demands of others. Setting boundaries can be challenging, often requiring us to assert our needs and say "no" when necessary. This can be particularly difficult for those who are naturally empathetic or who fear conflict. However, without clear boundaries, we risk being taken advantage of, feeling resentful, and ultimately, burning out. Learning to communicate our boundaries assertively and respectfully is an act of self-care, allowing us to prioritize our emotional health and maintain healthy relationships.

Self-regulation is not an innate talent but a skill that can be cultivated and honed through consistent practice.

Deep breathing exercises provide a physiological anchor, grounding us in the present moment amidst emotional storms.

Distraction techniques offer a psychological escape route, interrupting the cycle of negative thoughts and allowing us to regain perspective.

Setting boundaries serves as a preventative measure, protecting our emotional well-being and preventing us from being constantly overwhelmed.

By incorporating these strategies into our daily lives, we can gradually learn to tame the emotional beast within, navigating the complexities of life with greater resilience, clarity, and ultimately, achieving a greater sense of inner peace. The journey to self-mastery is a lifelong pursuit, but with each mindful breath, each chosen distraction, and each firmly established boundary, we move closer to becoming the masters of our own emotions.

Emotional intelligence is the alchemy of the soul, transforming the lead of reactive impulses into the gold of conscious responses, teaching us that true power lies not in the suppression of feelings, but in their wise and compassionate integration into the fabric of our lives, both personal and collective.

STEPPING INTO SOMEONE ELSE'S SHOES
The Profound Power of Empathy

Empathy, the ability to understand and share the feelings of another, is more than just a desirable trait; it is a fundamental building block of human connection, understanding, and progress. It's about transcending our own limited experiences and stepping into the shoes of another, seeing the world through their eyes, and feeling, to some degree, what they feel. This capacity to connect on a deeper level allows us to navigate the complexities of human relationships, foster compassion, and ultimately, create a more just and harmonious world.

Empathy is not a monolithic concept. While often used interchangeably with sympathy, empathy goes beyond feeling sorry for someone. It involves understanding *why* they feel that way, considering their circumstances, and acknowledging the validity of their experience. This nuanced understanding can be broken down into three key components: cognitive empathy, emotional empathy, and compassionate empathy. Cognitive empathy, also known as perspective-taking, allows us to understand another person's viewpoint and thought process. We can anticipate their reactions, predict their needs, and tailor our communication accordingly. Emotional empathy, on the other hand, involves experiencing the emotions of another person vicariously. We literally "feel" their sadness, joy, or frustration, allowing us to connect on a deeply human level. Finally, compassionate empathy goes beyond understanding and feeling; it compels us to act in a way that alleviates suffering and supports the other person. It is the bridge between understanding and action, driving us to help those in need.

Developing empathy is not an innate ability for everyone; often, it requires conscious effort and practice. Fortunately, there are concrete strategies we can employ to cultivate this crucial skill. Active listening is perhaps the most fundamental. This involves truly paying attention — not just hearing the words someone is saying, but also observing their non-verbal cues, such as body language and tone of voice. Reflecting back their feelings, paraphrasing their points, and asking clarifying questions demonstrates that we are genuinely engaged and striving to understand their perspective.

Furthermore, asking open-ended questions is crucial for fostering meaningful dialogue and encouraging others to share their thoughts and feelings. Questions that require more than a simple "yes" or "no" answer create space for vulnerability and deeper exploration. Instead of asking, "Are you okay?" try, "How are you really feeling about all of this?" This subtle shift in phrasing can encourage someone to open up and share their experiences with greater honesty and depth.

Another vital step in cultivating empathy is suspending judgment. It's easy to fall into the trap of making assumptions or criticizing others based on our own preconceived notions. However, genuine empathy requires us to put aside our judgments and biases and approach each interaction with an open mind. By focusing on understanding their perspective, rather than evaluating it, we create a safe space for vulnerability and connection.

Finally, and perhaps most challenging, is the practice of perspective-taking. This involves actively trying to see the world from someone else's point of view, even if we disagree with them. It requires us to consider their background, experiences, and beliefs, and to acknowledge that their perspective is just as valid as our own. This doesn't necessarily mean we have to agree with their views, but it does mean we need to understand them. By actively seeking out different perspectives, we can broaden our own understanding of the world and develop a deeper appreciation for the complexities of the human experience.

Empathy is not just a soft skill; it is a crucial component of effective communication, strong relationships, and a thriving society. By actively listening, asking open-ended questions, suspending judgment, and practicing perspective-taking, we can cultivate this essential ability and step into the shoes of another. In doing so, we not only enrich our own lives but also contribute to a more compassionate and understanding world for all. The ability to truly see and understand another person is a powerful force, capable of breaking down barriers, fostering connection, and ultimately, making the world a better place.

SELF-AWARENESS
The Foundation
of Emotional Intelligence

In the intricate tapestry of human interaction, emotional intelligence (EI) emerges as a vital thread, weaving together understanding, empathy, and effective communication. At the very heart of this intricate skill lies self-awareness, the cornerstone upon which all other aspects of EI are built. Self-awareness, fundamentally, is the ability to understand oneself – to recognize one's emotions, values, strengths, weaknesses, and, crucially, to understand how one's actions impact others. Without this foundational element, individuals are, as the saying goes, navigating life blindfolded, susceptible to impulsive decisions, strained relationships, and ultimately, a diminished capacity for personal and professional success.

To truly grasp the significance of self-awareness, one must consider its multifaceted nature. It begins with recognizing our emotions as they arise, not suppressing or ignoring them, but labeling and understanding their origins. Are we feeling anger because of a perceived injustice? Is our anxiety rooted in fear of failure? By consciously acknowledging these feelings, we gain control over them, preventing emotional reactivity from dictating our behavior. This ability to discern and articulate our emotional state is a crucial first step towards self-mastery.

Furthermore, self-awareness extends beyond the immediate emotional response. It requires introspection into our deeply held values and beliefs. What principles guide our decisions? What do we stand for? Understanding our core values provides a compass, guiding us to make choices that align with our true selves and contribute to a sense of purpose and fulfillment. When we act in accordance with our values, we experience greater authenticity, leading to increased self-esteem and stronger relationships.

Equally important is the ability to identify our strengths and weaknesses. Recognizing our areas of competence allows us to leverage our skills effectively, choose career paths that suit our talents, and contribute meaningfully to our communities. Conversely, acknowledging our weaknesses is not a sign of inadequacy but an opportunity for growth. By identifying areas where we struggle, we can seek support, develop new skills, or delegate tasks to others, ultimately becoming more well-rounded and effective individuals.

However, the most critical aspect of self-awareness lies in understanding the impact of our actions on others. This involves considering how our words, behaviors, and even non-verbal cues are perceived by those around us. Are we unintentionally coming across as dismissive or arrogant? Is our communication style hindering effective collaboration? This requires empathy and the ability to step outside of our own perspective and consider the experiences and feelings of others. Without this awareness, we risk damaging relationships, creating misunderstandings, and hindering our ability to build trust and rapport.

The absence of self-awareness can have profound consequences. Individuals lacking this crucial skill often struggle with self-regulation, leading to impulsive reactions and poor decision-making. They may be prone to blaming others for their mistakes, unable to accept responsibility for their actions. Their relationships may be strained by a lack of empathy and an inability to understand differing perspectives. In the professional realm, a lack of self-awareness can hinder career advancement, leading to conflicts with colleagues, difficulty in accepting feedback, and an inability to effectively manage teams.

Cultivating self-awareness is not a passive process; it requires conscious effort and dedication. Practices such as mindfulness meditation, journaling, and seeking feedback from trusted sources can significantly enhance our understanding of ourselves. Mindfulness allows us to observe our thoughts and emotions without judgment, creating space for reflection and insight. Journaling provides a platform to explore our experiences, identify patterns in our behavior, and gain clarity on our values and goals. Seeking feedback, while potentially uncomfortable, offers valuable insights into how we are perceived by others and can help us identify blind spots in our self-assessment.

Self-awareness is not merely a desirable trait; it is the foundational element of emotional intelligence and a critical ingredient for personal and professional success. It is the ability to understand our emotions, values, strengths, and weaknesses, and to recognize the impact of our actions on others. By cultivating self-awareness, we empower ourselves to make informed decisions, build strong relationships, and navigate life with greater purpose and effectiveness. In a world that often prioritizes external achievement, mastering self-awareness is a powerful act of self-discovery and a pathway to a more fulfilling and meaningful life.

EMOTIONAL INTELLIGENCE IN LEADERSHIP DEVELOPMENT

Understanding Emotional Intelligence

Emotional intelligence (EI) represents a critical skill set that encompasses the ability to recognize, understand, and manage our own emotions while also being attuned to the emotions of others. This multifaceted construct is increasingly recognized as essential not only in personal relationships but also in professional environments, particularly in leadership development. Leaders equipped with high emotional intelligence can foster a culture of empathy and collaboration, creating an atmosphere where team members feel valued and understood. In the realm of leadership, emotional intelligence can bridge the gap between authority and approachability, ultimately enhancing team dynamics and productivity.

In the field of mental health therapy, humanistic approaches prioritize the emotional experiences of individuals, emphasizing the importance of empathy, authenticity, and unconditional positive regard. Therapists who cultivate emotional intelligence can better connect with their clients, facilitating a safe space for healing. By understanding their own emotional responses and those of their clients, therapists can navigate complex emotional landscapes, promoting deeper insights and transformative experiences. This empathetic engagement aligns with the broader goals of humanistic psychology, which seeks to empower individuals through self-awareness and emotional growth.

Conflict resolution is another area where emotional intelligence plays a pivotal role. Understanding the emotions driving conflict allows individuals to address underlying issues rather than merely the surface disagreements. Practitioners skilled in emotional intelligence can mediate disputes by fostering open communication, validating feelings, and guiding parties toward collaborative solutions. This approach not only resolves conflicts but also strengthens relationships, paving the way for ongoing cooperation and understanding. In this context, emotional intelligence acts as a tool for social harmony, aligning with the values of social justice that seek equitable and peaceful resolutions.

In business ethics, emotional intelligence contributes significantly to wisdom-based decision-making. Leaders and decision-makers who incorporate emotional awareness into their processes are better equipped to consider the broader implications of their choices. This holistic perspective encourages a focus on well-being and the common good, rather than solely profit-driven motives. By integrating emotional intelligence into corporate culture, organizations can create environments that prioritize ethical considerations, employee morale, and social responsibility, fostering a sense of shared purpose among stakeholders.

Emotional intelligence is integral to community building and parenting techniques. By nurturing emotional awareness and empathy in both community settings and family dynamics, individuals can promote a culture of respect, cooperation, and shared values. Parents who model emotional intelligence can instill these principles in their children, preparing them to navigate social relationships with compassion and understanding. This foundational emotional awareness contributes to a more just and equitable society, reinforcing the essence of humanistic psychology in social justice movements. By recognizing and cultivating emotional intelligence across various dimensions of life, we can work towards a more empathetic and interconnected community.

The Role *of* EI *in* Effective Leadership

The role of emotional intelligence (EI) in effective leadership is increasingly recognized as a critical component in fostering environments where individuals can thrive. Emotional intelligence encompasses the ability to recognize, understand, and manage one's own emotions while also empathizing with others. In leadership contexts, this capacity enables leaders to connect with their teams on a deeper level, facilitating trust and collaboration. By prioritizing emotional intelligence, leaders can create a culture that values open communication and mutual respect, essential elements for any successful organization or social justice movement.

Effective leaders leverage their emotional intelligence to navigate complex interpersonal dynamics. They are adept at recognizing the emotional climate of their teams, allowing them to respond appropriately to conflicts and challenges. This sensitivity not only aids in conflict resolution but also enhances team cohesion. Leaders who demonstrate high EI are more capable of fostering an inclusive environment where diverse perspectives are valued, ultimately leading to more innovative solutions and a stronger commitment to shared goals.

Emotional intelligence is integral to wisdom-based decision-making in business ethics. Leaders who possess EI are more likely to consider the emotional and ethical implications of their choices, aligning their decisions with the greater good. This thoughtful approach to leadership contributes to a more sustainable business model, reinforcing the notion that success should not solely be measured by profit but also by the positive impact on employees, communities, and the environment. Such leaders inspire others to prioritize ethical considerations in their decision-making processes, fostering a culture of integrity and accountability.

In the context of community building, emotional intelligence serves as a foundational element in enhancing social values. Leaders who are emotionally intelligent are better equipped to engage with their communities, understanding the unique challenges and needs of diverse groups. By cultivating empathy and active listening, these leaders can bridge gaps and foster connections that empower individuals. This participatory approach not only strengthens community ties but also aligns with humanistic principles that prioritize the well-being of all members, creating a more equitable society.

Integrating emotional intelligence into parenting techniques can further enrich the development of future leaders. Parents who model emotional awareness and empathy instill these crucial skills in their children, preparing them to navigate the complexities of interpersonal relationships. As these children grow into adults, their emotional intelligence will serve as a vital asset in their personal and professional lives, promoting effective leadership that embodies humanistic values. By recognizing the role of emotional intelligence in leadership development, we can cultivate a generation of leaders committed to fostering social justice, community well-being, and ethical decision-making.

CASE STUDIES OF "EI" IN LEADERSHIP

Case studies of emotional intelligence (EI) in leadership provide valuable insights into how leaders can effectively navigate complex social dynamics and foster environments that promote well-being and collaboration. One notable example is the leadership style of Satya Nadella, CEO of Microsoft. Upon taking the helm, Nadella emphasized empathy as a core value within the company, transforming Microsoft's culture from a competitive, cutthroat environment to one that values collaboration and innovation. His approach illustrates how EI can be instrumental in cultivating a workplace culture that prioritizes emotional awareness and understanding, ultimately leading to enhanced employee engagement and organizational success.

- Another compelling case study is the work of **Howard Schultz**, former CEO of Starbucks. Schultz's leadership was characterized by a strong commitment to community values and social responsibility, which he integrated into the company's business model. By prioritizing the emotional and social needs of both employees and customers, Schultz created a sense of belonging and purpose within the organization. His focus on EI not only improved workplace morale but also positioned Starbucks as a leader in ethical business practices, demonstrating how humanistic approaches can drive both profitability and positive social change.

- In the realm of conflict resolution, the leadership of **Nelson Mandela** offers profound lessons on EI. Mandela's ability to empathize with both his supporters and opponents facilitated a peaceful transition from apartheid to democracy in South Africa. His emphasis on understanding the emotions and perspectives of others allowed him to forge alliances and foster reconciliation in a deeply divided society. This case underscores the importance of emotional intelligence in leadership, particularly in navigating conflicts and building coalitions that transcend individual interests for the common good.

- The case of **Jacinda Ardern**, former Prime Minister of New Zealand, highlights the role of EI in crisis management. Ardern's response to the Christchurch mosque shootings in 2019 showcased her ability to connect with the emotions of her constituents, offering compassion and solidarity during a time of national mourning. Her leadership style, marked by transparency and empathy, not only reassured the public but also encouraged collective healing and resilience. This example reinforces the notion that emotionally intelligent leadership is vital in addressing societal challenges and strengthening community bonds.

The integration of EI in parenting techniques is illustrated through the work of experts like Daniel Goleman, who emphasizes the impact of emotionally intelligent parenting on children's development. Leaders in family dynamics who practice EI foster environments where children learn to express and manage their emotions effectively. This approach not only nurtures individual well-being but also cultivates future leaders who understand the importance of empathy and social values in their interactions. The connection between emotional intelligence in leadership and parenting highlights a holistic approach to human development, reinforcing the idea that nurturing emotional skills can lead to broader societal benefits.

HUMANISTIC APPROACHES TO MENTAL HEALTH THERAPY

Principles of Humanistic Therapy

Humanistic therapy is grounded in several key principles that collectively emphasize the inherent worth and potential of individuals. At its core, this therapeutic approach is rooted in the belief that people are fundamentally good and possess an innate capacity for self-actualization. This perspective fosters an environment where individuals can explore their feelings, thoughts, and behaviors without fear of judgment. By prioritizing the subjective experience of clients, humanistic therapy encourages a deeper understanding of oneself, which is essential in various contexts, including leadership development and conflict resolution.

One of the primary principles of humanistic therapy is the concept of empathy. Empathy involves fully understanding and reflecting the emotions and experiences of another, which is crucial in establishing a therapeutic relationship. In leadership development, leaders who practice empathy can create a more inclusive and supportive workplace culture. This principle also plays a vital role in conflict resolution, as empathetic leaders are better equipped to understand differing perspectives and facilitate constructive dialogue among conflicting parties. By fostering empathy, humanistic therapy contributes to more effective communication and collaboration in various social settings.

Another essential principle is unconditional positive regard, which refers to accepting and valuing individuals without conditions or judgments. This principle encourages clients to feel safe and accepted as they navigate their personal challenges. In the context of parenting techniques, incorporating unconditional positive regard can strengthen the parent-child relationship, promoting emotional intelligence in children. When children feel accepted for who they are, they are more likely to develop healthy self-esteem and the ability to empathize with others, which are critical components of emotional intelligence.

Self-awareness and personal responsibility are also fundamental tenets of humanistic therapy. Clients are encouraged to explore their thoughts, feelings, and behaviors to gain insight into their motivations and choices. This principle is particularly relevant in the realm of wisdom-based decision-making in business ethics. Leaders who cultivate self-awareness are more likely to make ethical decisions that consider the well-being of their employees and the broader community. By taking responsibility for their actions, individuals can foster a culture of accountability, ultimately contributing to social justice movements and community building.

Humanistic therapy emphasizes the importance of personal growth and self-actualization. This principle aligns with redefining success through well-being and common good principles. Rather than merely achieving external markers of success, individuals are encouraged to pursue personal fulfillment and contribute positively to society. By prioritizing personal growth and the betterment of communities, humanistic therapy not only enhances individual well-being but also supports broader social justice initiatives. This holistic approach underscores the interconnectedness of personal and collective growth, reinforcing the role of humanistic psychology in fostering a more equitable and compassionate society.

Impact on Individual
and Community Well-Being

The impact on individual and community well-being is multifaceted, reflecting the interconnectedness of personal mental health and broader social dynamics. Humanistic psychology emphasizes the inherent value of each individual, positing that personal growth and self-actualization contribute significantly to the well-being of communities. When individuals are supported in their emotional and psychological needs, they are more likely to engage positively with their communities, fostering environments of empathy, cooperation, and resilience. This synergy between individual well-being and community health is crucial for fostering social justice and equitable practices.

Emotional intelligence plays a pivotal role in enhancing both individual and communal well-being. Leaders who cultivate emotional intelligence can navigate the complexities of human relationships and social interactions more effectively. By recognizing and managing emotions—both their own and those of others—leaders are better equipped to foster inclusive environments that prioritize mental health and collective welfare. In workplaces, emotionally intelligent leaders can create cultures of trust and collaboration, which not only improve employee satisfaction but also contribute to higher productivity and innovative problem-solving.

In the context of mental health therapy, humanistic approaches that prioritize empathy, genuine connection, and self-exploration have profound implications for individual well-being. These therapeutic practices encourage individuals to understand and express their emotions, enabling them to develop healthier coping mechanisms and build resilience. As individuals heal and grow, they can contribute positively to their communities, creating ripple effects that enhance collective well-being. Furthermore, when communities embrace humanistic principles in mental health, they cultivate environments that prioritize emotional support and reduce stigma, leading to a healthier societal framework.

The integration of emotional intelligence into parenting techniques is another critical factor in promoting well-being at both individual and community levels. Parents who model and teach emotional awareness and regulation equip their children with essential life skills that foster positive relationships and social responsibility. This generational transfer of emotional intelligence not only improves family dynamics but also contributes to the development of compassionate and socially aware citizens. As these children grow into adults, they carry forward the values of empathy and cooperation, reinforcing community bonds and enhancing social cohesion.

Redefining success through well-being and common good principles necessitates a shift in societal values. Communities that prioritize emotional intelligence and humanistic approaches to social interactions create environments where individuals can thrive. This holistic view of success emphasizes not just personal achievement, but also the collective health of the community. By committing to these principles, societies can foster an inclusive atmosphere that supports the well-being of all members, thereby achieving greater social justice and equity.

Integrating Humanistic Approaches in Practice

Integrating humanistic approaches in practice involves a conscious effort to place human values and dignity at the forefront of various fields, particularly in psychology, leadership, and community development. Humanistic psychology emphasizes the importance of personal growth, self-actualization, and the intrinsic worth of every individual. By applying these principles, professionals can create environments that promote emotional intelligence, foster healthy relationships, and cultivate a sense of belonging among community members. This integration is not just theoretical; it requires actionable strategies that can be implemented in everyday practices.

In the realm of leadership development, humanistic approaches encourage leaders to develop emotional intelligence as a core competency. This involves understanding and managing one's own emotions, as well as recognizing and responding to the emotions of others. A leader grounded in humanistic principles is more likely to prioritize collaboration, empathy, and ethical decision-making. Such leaders can create a positive workplace culture where employees feel valued and understood, ultimately leading to increased engagement and productivity. By fostering an emotionally intelligent leadership style, organizations can better navigate conflicts and enhance overall workplace dynamics.

Mental health therapy also greatly benefits from integrating humanistic approaches. Therapists who adhere to these principles prioritize client-centered care, focusing on the individual's experiences and emotional needs. This method encourages clients to explore their feelings in a safe environment, promoting healing and personal growth. As mental health practitioners embrace humanistic values, they can address the broader social determinants of health, contributing to social justice by ensuring equitable access to mental health services. This holistic approach not only aids individual clients but can also influence community health outcomes.

In the context of community building, humanistic approaches can strengthen social values and promote collective well-being. Initiatives that prioritize empathy, inclusivity, and mutual respect can lead to stronger, more resilient communities. By encouraging dialogue and understanding among diverse groups, humanistic principles can help resolve conflicts and bridge divides. This process not only enhances social cohesion but also empowers individuals to take an active role in their communities, fostering a culture of participation and shared responsibility.

Redefining success through well-being and common good principles is essential in today's rapidly changing world. Humanistic approaches challenge traditional metrics of success, advocating for a broader definition that includes emotional health and community welfare. By emphasizing collective well-being over individual achievement, organizations and leaders can create sustainable practices that benefit not only their immediate stakeholders but society at large. This reorientation towards a more humanistic vision of success can inspire individuals and communities to pursue goals that reflect their values and contribute to the common good.

THE ROLE OF EMOTIONAL INTELLIGENCE IN CONFLICT RESOLUTION
Understanding Conflict Dynamics

Conflict is an inherent aspect of human interaction, often arising from differing values, beliefs, and interests. To navigate conflict effectively, it is essential to understand its dynamics, which encompass the emotional, psychological, and social factors at play. Conflicts can escalate when individuals lack the emotional intelligence to recognize their own feelings and those of others. By appreciating the underlying reasons for conflict, leaders and practitioners can foster environments where dialogue replaces discord, ultimately leading to constructive resolutions that align with humanistic principles.

At the core of conflict dynamics is the recognition that emotions significantly influence behavior. Emotional intelligence allows individuals to manage their responses, empathize with others, and communicate effectively. In leadership development, fostering emotional intelligence serves as a critical tool for conflict resolution. Leaders equipped with this skill can assess the emotional landscape of a situation, identify triggers, and intervene in a way that respects the perspectives of all parties involved. This approach not only de-escalates tensions but also promotes a culture of understanding and collaboration.

Furthermore, conflicts often reflect deeper societal issues, such as inequality and injustice. Humanistic psychology emphasizes the importance of addressing these systemic factors to achieve true resolution. By integrating emotional intelligence into social justice movements, individuals can better articulate their experiences and grievances while also listening to the narratives of others. This dual approach fosters a more inclusive dialogue, allowing for a more profound understanding of the issues at hand and paving the way for collective action that seeks the common good.

In the context of community building, understanding conflict dynamics is essential for enhancing social values. Communities thrive when members can navigate disagreements thoughtfully and respectfully. By promoting emotional intelligence in community initiatives, individuals learn to appreciate diverse viewpoints and work toward shared goals. This process not only strengthens interpersonal relationships but also cultivates a sense of belonging and solidarity, which are crucial for sustainable social change.

Redefining success in business and personal development requires an acknowledgment of the role emotional intelligence plays in conflict dynamics. Organizations that prioritize well-being and common good principles create environments where conflicts are viewed as opportunities for growth rather than obstacles. Leaders who embrace this mindset can foster a workplace culture that values emotional intelligence, ultimately leading to improved morale, productivity, and innovation. In this way, the understanding of conflict dynamics becomes a vital component of not only resolving disagreements but also nurturing a more compassionate and equitable society.

USING "*EI*"
to De-escalate Tensions

Emotional intelligence (EI) plays a crucial role in de-escalating tensions in various contexts, including workplaces, community settings, and personal relationships. Understanding and managing emotions, both in oneself and in others, allows individuals to navigate conflicts more effectively. This skill set is particularly vital in environments where stress and misunderstandings can lead to heightened emotions. By recognizing the emotional undercurrents in a situation, leaders and individuals can respond with empathy and clarity, fostering a more constructive dialogue.

One of the key components of emotional intelligence is self-awareness. Leaders who are attuned to their feelings can better assess how their emotions influence their reactions and decision-making processes. When faced with conflict, self-aware individuals can take a step back, evaluate their emotional responses, and choose a course of action that prioritizes resolution over escalation. This introspection not only aids personal management but also sets a tone for others, encouraging a culture of reflection and understanding rather than one dominated by reactive behaviors.

Empathy, another pillar of emotional intelligence, is essential for de-escalation. By genuinely understanding the perspectives and feelings of others, individuals can create a safe space for open communication. When people feel heard and validated, they are less likely to react defensively. This empathetic approach can diffuse tension, allowing for collaborative problem-solving rather than adversarial confrontation. In practice, this means actively listening, acknowledging emotions, and showing that one values the other person's viewpoint, which can pave the way for mutual understanding.

Effective communication is integral to leveraging emotional intelligence in conflict resolution. Articulating thoughts and feelings in a clear and respectful manner helps to minimize misunderstandings that can lead to conflict. EI enhances one's ability to express needs and concerns without assigning blame, thereby fostering a more constructive dialogue. Furthermore, incorporating techniques such as nonverbal cues and active listening can reinforce a message of understanding and respect, further promoting a calm and cooperative atmosphere.

Incorporating emotional intelligence into community building enhances social values that contribute to collective well-being. When individuals in a community prioritize emotional awareness and regulation, they create an environment where collaboration flourishes. This sense of shared emotional responsibility can lead to more effective conflict resolution and a stronger commitment to common goals. As communities embrace these principles, they not only navigate tensions with greater ease but also redefine success in terms of collective well-being and social harmony, ultimately advancing the broader aims of social justice movements.

STRATEGIES
for Conflict Resolution

Strategies for conflict resolution are essential for fostering understanding and cooperation in various contexts, including workplaces, communities, and personal relationships. Effective conflict resolution hinges on the application of emotional intelligence, which involves recognizing, understanding, and managing emotions in oneself and others. By cultivating emotional awareness and empathy, leaders and individuals can create an environment conducive to open dialogue and constructive problem-solving. This approach aligns with humanistic principles, emphasizing the inherent worth of each person and the value of collaborative efforts.

One effective strategy involves active listening, which requires participants to fully engage with one another's perspectives without judgment. This technique not only demonstrates respect but also allows for a deeper understanding of the underlying issues at play. By paraphrasing and summarizing what the other party has expressed, individuals can clarify misunderstandings and validate feelings. In this process, emotional intelligence plays a critical role, as it enables individuals to remain calm and focused, even in the face of disagreement. This practice fosters a sense of safety that encourages open communication and reduces the likelihood of escalation.

Another strategy is to identify common goals or values that can serve as a foundation for resolution. When conflicting parties recognize shared interests or aspirations, it becomes easier to navigate disagreements. This approach not only reduces tension but also highlights the importance of collaboration, reinforcing the belief that working together can lead to mutually beneficial outcomes. Leaders who demonstrate emotional intelligence can facilitate this process by guiding discussions toward shared objectives and ensuring that all voices are heard, thereby fostering a sense of community.

Involving a neutral third party can also be an effective strategy for conflict resolution. Mediators, trained in emotional intelligence and conflict resolution techniques, can help facilitate discussions and provide an objective perspective. They can assist in ensuring that all parties feel respected and understood, helping to diffuse any heightened emotions that may be present. This strategy not only aids in resolving the immediate conflict but also serves as a learning opportunity for all involved, as they witness firsthand the benefits of collaborative dialogue and emotional regulation.

Fostering a culture of emotional intelligence within organizations and communities can lead to more sustainable conflict resolution practices. This can be achieved through training and development programs that emphasize emotional awareness, empathy, and effective communication. When emotional intelligence becomes a core value, individuals are more likely to approach conflicts with a mindset geared toward understanding and cooperation. By integrating these strategies, organizations and communities can build stronger relationships, enhance their social values, and work collectively toward the common good, thereby embodying the principles of humanism in action.

To cultivate a society where emotional intelligence flourishes is to build a sanctuary for the human spirit, a space where the unspoken language of the heart is honored, where vulnerabilities are not weaknesses but bridges to deeper connection, and where the symphony of feelings is understood as the very music of our shared humanity.

WISDOM BASED DECISION MAKING
IN BUSINESS ETHICS
Defining Wisdom in Business Contexts

Defining wisdom in business contexts requires a nuanced understanding that transcends traditional definitions. Wisdom is often associated with knowledge and experience, but in a business setting, it encompasses the capacity to make sound judgments that consider not only the immediate outcomes but also the broader social implications. This form of wisdom integrates emotional intelligence, ethical considerations, and an awareness of the interconnectedness of stakeholders, thereby fostering an environment where decisions are made with the common good in mind. In this context, wisdom becomes a critical component of leadership, influencing how leaders approach challenges and guide their teams.

Incorporating emotional intelligence into the definition of wisdom in business is essential. Emotional intelligence encompasses self-awareness, empathy, and relational skills, all of which are vital for effective decision-making. Leaders who possess emotional intelligence are better equipped to navigate complex interpersonal dynamics, leading to more thoughtful and inclusive decisions. This capability not only enhances workplace culture but also promotes a sense of community and shared purpose among employees. As leaders develop their emotional intelligence, they cultivate a wisdom that enables them to align organizational goals with the well-being of their teams and communities.

Wisdom in business contexts involves ethical decision-making that prioritizes long-term benefits over short-term gains. This perspective is crucial in an increasingly interconnected world where corporate actions can have significant social implications. Leaders who embrace a wisdom-based approach recognize the importance of ethical considerations in their strategies, ensuring that their organizations contribute positively to society. This commitment to ethical behavior fosters trust and loyalty among stakeholders, further enhancing the reputation and sustainability of the business.

Community building is another vital aspect of wisdom in business. Leaders who understand the importance of social values are better positioned to create inclusive environments that empower individuals and groups. By promoting collaboration and respect, these leaders can foster a sense of belonging and shared responsibility among employees, customers, and the broader community. This focus on community not only enhances workplace culture but also aligns business practices with the principles of social justice, ultimately driving positive change.

In summary, defining wisdom in business contexts involves a multifaceted approach that integrates emotional intelligence, ethical decision-making, and community building. By emphasizing these elements, leaders can redefine success to encompass not just financial metrics but also the well-being of individuals and society as a whole. This holistic view of wisdom not only contributes to more effective leadership but also resonates with the principles of humanism, ensuring that businesses operate in a manner that supports social justice and the greater good.

The Impact of EI *on* Ethical Decision Making

The integration of emotional intelligence (EI) into ethical decision-making processes has profound implications across various domains, including leadership, mental health, and community building. Emotional intelligence, characterized by the ability to recognize, understand, and manage one's own emotions and the emotions of others, serves as a critical tool for navigating complex ethical dilemmas. In contexts such as leadership development and workplace culture, EI fosters an environment where ethical considerations are prioritized, leading to decisions that reflect a commitment to social justice and the common good.

Leaders equipped with high emotional intelligence are better positioned to approach ethical challenges with empathy and insight. They are more likely to consider the perspectives and feelings of diverse stakeholders, which is essential for making decisions that are not only rational but also morally sound. This empathetic perspective encourages a culture of openness and trust, essential components for ethical dialogue and collaborative problem-solving within organizations. As leaders model EI in their decision-making, they set a precedent for their teams, reinforcing the importance of ethical considerations in everyday practices.

In the realm of mental health therapy, humanistic approaches benefit significantly from emotional intelligence. Therapists who possess EI can better connect with clients, fostering an environment conducive to open communication and trust. This connection is vital for ethical practice, as it allows therapists to navigate sensitive issues with compassion and respect. By understanding the emotional states of their clients, therapists can tailor their interventions to promote well-being while adhering to ethical standards. This alignment of emotional intelligence with therapeutic practice enhances the ethical decision-making process, ensuring that client welfare remains the focal point.

The role of EI in conflict resolution further highlights its impact on ethical decision-making. Conflicts often arise from misunderstandings or emotional responses that cloud judgment. Individuals who practice emotional intelligence can de-escalate tensions by recognizing and validating the emotions involved. This approach not only resolves conflicts more effectively but also promotes ethical outcomes, as decisions made in a calm and empathetic environment are likely to consider the broader implications for all parties involved. By prioritizing emotional understanding, individuals can arrive at solutions that honor the dignity and rights of everyone affected.

The principles of wisdom-based decision-making in business ethics illustrate the potential of emotional intelligence to redefine success. In a business environment increasingly focused on social responsibility, leaders who integrate EI into their decision-making processes are more likely to prioritize ethical outcomes over mere profit. This shift not only enhances workplace culture but also contributes to community well-being by aligning organizational goals with societal values. As organizations recognize the importance of emotional intelligence in fostering ethical behavior, they pave the way for a more just and equitable society, demonstrating that success can and should be measured by the common good.

CASE STUDIES OF WISDOM-BASED APPROACHES

Case studies of wisdom-based approaches demonstrate the profound impact that emotional intelligence and humanistic principles can have across various domains, including leadership, mental health, and community development. In leadership development, organizations that emphasize emotional intelligence have reported significant improvements in team dynamics and decision-making processes.

- One notable case is a non-profit organization that implemented a leadership program focused on empathy and active listening. Leaders who participated exhibited enhanced ability to connect with their teams, resulting in increased morale and productivity. This case underscores how wisdom-based approaches can transform traditional leadership models into more inclusive and effective frameworks.

In the realm of mental health therapy, humanistic approaches rooted in wisdom have proven effective in facilitating deeper client engagement and personal growth.

- A community mental health center adopted a wisdom-based therapeutic model that prioritized the therapeutic alliance and client autonomy. By integrating mindfulness practices and empathetic communication into therapy sessions, therapists observed a marked improvement in clients' emotional regulation and resilience. This case illustrates how fostering emotional intelligence in therapeutic settings not only aids in healing but also empowers individuals to navigate their challenges more effectively.

Conflict resolution strategies that incorporate emotional intelligence and wisdom have shown to be instrumental in de-escalating tensions and fostering understanding in diverse settings.

- A prominent educational institution utilized a restorative justice framework to address conflicts among students. By training facilitators to employ empathy and active listening, the program created a safe space for dialogue. Participants reported feeling heard and respected, which led to more constructive outcomes and strengthened relationships. This case emphasizes the potential of wisdom-based approaches to transform conflict into opportunities for growth and reconciliation.

In business ethics, organizations that embrace wisdom-based decision-making have navigated complex moral dilemmas more successfully.

- A multinational corporation adopted a values-driven approach in its corporate governance, focusing on transparency and stakeholder engagement. By implementing a decision-making process that included diverse perspectives and ethical considerations, the company not only enhanced its reputation but also built trust with its employees and customers. This case highlights the importance of integrating emotional intelligence and humanistic values into business practices, ultimately redefining success in terms of long-term social impact rather than short-term profits.

Community building initiatives that prioritize enhanced social values illustrate the power of wisdom-based approaches in fostering unity and resilience.

- A grassroots organization launched a program aimed at promoting social cohesion through shared community experiences. By creating spaces for dialogue, collaboration, and collective problem-solving, participants developed stronger social bonds and a shared sense of purpose. This case exemplifies how wisdom-driven community initiatives can cultivate an environment where emotional intelligence thrives, leading to sustainable community development and social justice.

COMMUNITY BUILDING THROUGH ENHANCED SOCIAL VALUES
The Role of Emotional Intelligence in Community Engagement

The role of emotional intelligence in community engagement is pivotal in fostering meaningful connections among individuals and groups. Emotional intelligence, defined as the ability to recognize, understand, and manage our own emotions while effectively navigating the emotions of others, serves as a foundation for building trust and collaboration within communities. When individuals possess high emotional intelligence, they are better equipped to empathize with diverse perspectives, which is essential in addressing the complex social issues that often arise in community settings. This capacity for empathy not only enhances interpersonal relationships but also creates an environment where all voices are valued and heard.

In the context of leadership development, emotional intelligence becomes a critical asset for those who seek to inspire and mobilize community members. Leaders who demonstrate emotional intelligence are adept at recognizing the emotional climate of their teams, allowing them to respond appropriately to the needs and concerns of others. This responsiveness not only fosters a sense of belonging but also encourages active participation from community members. By integrating emotional intelligence into leadership practices, leaders can cultivate a more inclusive atmosphere that promotes collaboration and shared decision-making, ultimately leading to more effective community engagement.

Emotional intelligence plays a significant role in conflict resolution within communities. Conflicts are inevitable in any social group, but how these conflicts are managed can determine the overall health of the community. Individuals with strong emotional intelligence can navigate disputes with a level of sensitivity that enables them to de-escalate tensions and facilitate constructive dialogue. This approach not only addresses the immediate issues at hand but also strengthens the community's resilience by fostering an environment where individuals feel safe to express their emotions and work towards common goals.

Incorporating emotional intelligence into community building efforts also enhances social values, such as compassion, respect, and cooperation. These values are essential for creating a supportive network that can address shared challenges effectively. By prioritizing emotional intelligence in community initiatives, organizations and leaders can promote a culture of understanding and collective well-being. This shift not only empowers individuals but also leads to stronger social bonds and an increased capacity for collective action, reinforcing the idea that community engagement is rooted in shared emotional experiences.

Finally, the integration of emotional intelligence into parenting techniques further reinforces its importance in community engagement. Parents who model emotional intelligence create a nurturing environment that encourages children to develop their own emotional skills. These children, in turn, are more likely to engage positively within their communities as they grow. By embedding emotional intelligence within the fabric of family life and community interactions, we can cultivate a generation that values empathy and collaboration, ultimately leading to stronger, more resilient communities grounded in social justice principles.

STRATEGIES
for Fostering Social Values

Strategies for fostering social values are essential for creating a more just and compassionate society. One effective strategy is the integration of emotional intelligence into leadership development. Leaders who possess high emotional intelligence are better equipped to understand and manage their own emotions, as well as those of their team members. This awareness fosters an environment where empathy and active listening are prioritized, allowing leaders to cultivate a culture of respect and collaboration. By modeling these behaviors, leaders can inspire others to adopt similar values, ultimately enhancing the social fabric of their organizations and communities.

Another vital strategy involves humanistic approaches to mental health therapy, emphasizing the importance of empathy, acceptance, and understanding in therapeutic settings. By fostering a therapeutic alliance built on trust and respect, therapists can empower individuals to explore their values and beliefs. This exploration not only aids personal growth but also encourages clients to consider their roles within larger social contexts. As individuals become more aware of their social responsibilities, they are likely to engage in behaviors that promote collective well-being, reinforcing the social values that underpin healthy communities.

In the sphere of conflict resolution, emotional intelligence plays a pivotal role in fostering social values. By enhancing our ability to recognize and manage emotions during conflicts, we can approach disputes with a mindset focused on collaboration rather than contention. Techniques such as active listening, empathy, and open communication can transform adversarial situations into opportunities for understanding and growth. When individuals approach conflict resolution with the intent to uphold shared values and seek common ground, they contribute to a culture of respect and cooperation that extends beyond individual interactions, benefiting the larger community.

Wisdom-based decision-making in business ethics is another strategy that can foster social values. By prioritizing ethical considerations and the common good over purely profit-driven motives, businesses can play a transformative role in society. Leaders who embrace a holistic view, considering the impact of their decisions on all stakeholders, are better positioned to cultivate an organizational culture that values integrity and social responsibility. This approach not only enhances the ethical standards of the business but also encourages employees to align their personal values with those of the organization, creating a unified commitment to positive social change.

Community building through enhanced social values requires intentional efforts to create spaces for dialogue and collaboration. Initiatives that promote inclusivity and diversity can strengthen community bonds by encouraging individuals from different backgrounds to share their experiences and perspectives. By fostering environments where social values are actively discussed and celebrated, communities can cultivate a shared sense of identity and purpose. Integrating emotional intelligence into parenting techniques further supports this effort, as parents who model empathy and respect can raise children who are attuned to the needs and feelings of others. Together, these strategies contribute to a holistic approach to fostering social values, ultimately leading to a more equitable and compassionate society.

SUCCESSFUL
Community Initiatives

Successful community initiatives often serve as a testament to the power of collective action and the application of humanistic principles in addressing social issues. These initiatives demonstrate that when individuals come together with a shared vision, they can create meaningful change that aligns with the values of emotional intelligence, empathy, and social responsibility. In many cases, these projects not only address immediate community needs but also foster a culture of collaboration and understanding that can have a lasting impact on social dynamics.

One exemplary model of a successful community initiative can be found in **community gardens**. These spaces not only provide fresh produce to neighborhoods with limited access to healthy food options but also serve as platforms for building social connections among diverse groups. Participants engage in cooperative gardening efforts, which require effective communication, conflict resolution, and emotional intelligence. As community members work side by side, they cultivate not just plants but also relationships, fostering an environment where shared values and collaborative problem-solving thrive.

Another notable example is the establishment of **local mental health support networks.** These initiatives often emerge in response to a growing awareness of mental health needs within communities. By integrating humanistic approaches to therapy, such networks prioritize the emotional well-being of individuals and emphasize the importance of peer support. Training volunteers in emotional intelligence skills enhances their ability to provide empathetic listening and guidance, creating a safe space for those in need. Such initiatives exemplify how community-driven efforts can lead to improved mental health outcomes while reinforcing the value of human connection.

Youth mentorship programs also illustrate the effectiveness of community initiatives in promoting social values and emotional intelligence. These programs connect young people with mentors who provide guidance, support, and encouragement, fostering an environment where emotional intelligence can flourish. Through these relationships, youth learn valuable life skills, such as effective communication and empathy, which are essential for their personal and professional development. By investing in the emotional growth of future generations, these initiatives contribute to the long-term success of communities and help redefine success in terms of well-being and mutual support.

Successful community initiatives often emphasize the importance of **inclusivity and diversity**. Programs that actively seek to engage marginalized groups not only enhance social cohesion but also enrich the overall community experience. By recognizing and valuing diverse perspectives, these initiatives promote a culture of respect and understanding, which is critical in addressing systemic issues. The integration of emotional intelligence into these efforts allows community leaders to navigate complex social dynamics, ensuring that all voices are heard and empowered. In this way, successful community initiatives not only serve immediate purposes but also lay the groundwork for sustainable social justice movements.

To truly comprehend the human experiment is to navigate the labyrinth of our feelings, a journey where the echoes of past joys and the shadows of past sorrows coalesce into the present, reminding us that the ephemeral nature of happiness and the enduring weight of grief are not opposing forces, but the twin pillars upon which our understanding of existence rests.

INTEGRATING EMOTIONAL INTELLIGENCE IN PARENTING TECHNIQUES

The Importance *of* EI in Parenting

The importance of emotional intelligence (EI) in parenting cannot be overstated, particularly in the context of fostering well-rounded, resilient individuals. Parenting is not merely about providing for physical needs; it involves nurturing emotional and social capacities that children will carry into adulthood. Emotional intelligence equips parents with the skills to recognize, understand, and manage their emotions as well as those of their children. This self-awareness and empathy are critical in creating an environment where children feel safe to express themselves, ultimately leading to healthier emotional development.

Effective parenting requires the ability to respond to a child's emotional needs with sensitivity. Parents who demonstrate high levels of emotional intelligence are more adept at recognizing when their children are distressed or overwhelmed. They can validate feelings and offer support, which helps children learn to navigate their own emotions. This responsive approach not only strengthens the parent-child bond but also models healthy emotional regulation, teaching children how to articulate their feelings and cope with challenges. Such modeling is essential in developing children who can thrive in various aspects of life, including their relationships and academic pursuits.

Moreover, integrating emotional intelligence into parenting techniques can significantly impact conflict resolution within the family. Disagreements are inevitable in any household, but parents equipped with EI can approach conflicts constructively. They are more likely to listen actively to their children's perspectives, facilitating discussions that promote understanding and compromise. This practice not only resolves immediate conflicts but also instills in children the skills to handle disagreements in their future relationships, contributing to a more harmonious family dynamic and fostering social skills that extend beyond the home.

In the broader context of community building, emotionally intelligent parenting contributes to the development of socially aware and empathetic citizens. Children raised in environments where emotional intelligence is prioritized are more likely to engage positively with others, embrace diversity, and advocate for social justice. They carry with them the values of empathy and cooperation, which are essential in creating inclusive communities. As these children grow into adults, their ability to connect with others and understand different perspectives can lead to a more just and equitable society.

The integration of emotional intelligence in parenting is not just about the immediate effects on children; it also influences the overall well-being of families. Parents who practice EI tend to experience lower levels of stress and higher satisfaction in their parenting roles. They create a nurturing atmosphere that fosters mutual respect and understanding. This environment not only benefits children but also contributes to the mental health and resilience of parents themselves. In this way, emotional intelligence serves as a foundational element in redefining success within families, emphasizing well-being and the common good over traditional metrics of achievement.

Techniques *for* Developing "*EI*" in Children

Techniques for developing emotional intelligence (EI) in children can be pivotal in shaping their ability to understand and manage emotions, both in themselves and in others.

One effective approach is through **modeling behaviors** that exemplify high emotional intelligence. Adults can demonstrate empathy, active listening, and effective communication in their daily interactions. When children observe these behaviors, they are more likely to replicate them. Engaging in discussions about emotions, such as naming feelings during different situations, can provide children with a vocabulary to express themselves and recognize the emotions of others. This practice not only supports emotional literacy but also lays the groundwork for emotional regulation.

Another crucial technique is **incorporating role-playing and storytelling into learning experiences**. These activities encourage children to step into others' shoes and explore various emotional scenarios. Through role-playing exercises, children can practice responding to different emotional situations, fostering their ability to empathize and resolve conflicts. Additionally, stories that highlight emotional experiences can be a powerful tool for discussing feelings and ethical dilemmas. This narrative approach helps children understand complex emotional responses and the impact of their choices on others, reinforcing the importance of compassion and community values.

Creating a safe and supportive environment is essential for nurturing emotional intelligence. Children thrive in spaces where they feel accepted and understood. Adults can foster such environments by encouraging open dialogue about feelings and affirming children's emotional expressions. This support allows children to explore their emotions without fear of judgment, leading to increased self-awareness and confidence in managing their feelings. Regular check-ins and opportunities for children to share their thoughts and emotions can strengthen their emotional resilience and promote a culture of trust and cooperation.

Integrating emotional intelligence training into school curricula can also significantly enhance children's EI development. Schools can implement programs that focus on social-emotional learning (SEL), which equips students with the skills needed to navigate interpersonal relationships effectively. Such programs often include lessons on self-regulation, empathy, and conflict resolution, all of which are integral to emotional intelligence. By making EI a fundamental part of education, children learn to apply these skills in various contexts, from classroom interactions to future workplace environments, thereby contributing to a more emotionally intelligent society.

Involving children in community service and cooperative activities can further develop their emotional intelligence. These experiences teach children the value of empathy, teamwork, and social responsibility. By engaging with diverse groups and facing real-world challenges, children learn to appreciate different perspectives and the importance of collective well-being. This practice not only enhances their emotional skills but also instills a sense of belonging and purpose, aligning with the principles of humanistic psychology and social justice. Through these techniques, children can grow into emotionally intelligent adults who contribute positively to their communities and workplaces.

CASE STUDIES OF SUCCESSFUL PARENTING APPROACHES

Case studies of successful parenting approaches reveal the profound impact of emotional intelligence and humanistic principles on child development and family dynamics.

- One notable example is the approach taken by the Jones family, who adopted a communicative and empathetic style of parenting. The Joneses placed a significant emphasis on open dialogue, encouraging their children to express their feelings and thoughts without fear of judgment. This environment not only fostered emotional intelligence in the children but also strengthened their relationships, equipping them with skills to navigate social interactions and conflicts effectively.

- Another instructive case is that of the Garcia family, who integrated mindfulness practices into their daily routines. By teaching their children to be present and aware of their emotions, the Garcias cultivated resilience and emotional regulation. This approach proved beneficial, particularly when the children faced challenges at school or in peer relationships. The emphasis on mindfulness not only supported their emotional development but also promoted a sense of community and understanding within the family unit, reflecting the values of humanistic psychology.

- The Patel family exemplifies the integration of emotional intelligence into conflict resolution strategies. When disagreements arose, the Patels encouraged their children to articulate their perspectives while also actively listening to others. This practice helped the children develop empathy and negotiation skills, allowing them to resolve conflicts amicably. By modeling this behavior, the Patels not only addressed immediate issues but also instilled a lifelong ability to handle disputes with compassion and wisdom, aligning with broader principles of social justice.

- In the Thompson household, a focus on community building through enhanced social values has shaped the children's outlook on the world. The Thompsons regularly engage in community service and discussions about social issues, promoting a sense of responsibility and interconnectedness. This approach has nurtured a generation of socially aware individuals who understand the importance of contributing to the common good. Their commitment to humanistic values has not only enriched their family life but has also empowered their children to become advocates for social change.

- The Nguyen family has redefined success through well-being and common good principles. Rather than emphasizing traditional metrics of achievement, such as grades or accolades, they celebrate emotional well-being and personal fulfillment. This focus has allowed their children to pursue their passions and develop a strong sense of self-worth independent of societal pressures. By prioritizing mental health and emotional intelligence, the Nguyens have created a supportive environment that encourages their children to thrive, embodying the essence of humanistic psychology in their parenting approach.

To navigate the human condition is to chart a course through the ever-shifting tides of feeling, where the ephemeral nature of joy and the enduring weight of sorrow teach us the profound truth that our capacity for both suffering and transcendence is the very measure of our humanity, a testament to the soul's resilience.

HUMANISTIC PSYCHOLOGY IN SOCIAL JUSTICE MOVEMENTS

Historical Overview *of* Humanistic Psychology

Humanistic psychology emerged in the mid-20th century as a significant response to the prevailing psychological paradigms of behaviorism and psychoanalysis. Founded by key figures such as Abraham Maslow and Carl Rogers, this movement emphasized the inherent worth of the individual and the importance of personal growth, self-actualization, and human potential. The historical context of this development is crucial, as it arose during a time of social upheaval and transformation, with the civil rights movement, counterculture, and various liberation movements influencing its principles. Humanistic psychology sought to address the complexities of human experience by focusing on subjective experiences and the individual's capacity for self-determination.

The philosophical underpinnings of humanistic psychology are rooted in existentialism and phenomenology, both of which prioritize personal experience and the search for meaning. This perspective shifted the focus from pathology to wellness, encouraging practitioners to explore the strengths and resources of clients rather than solely their weaknesses. This approach has had a profound influence on therapy modalities, resulting in more empathetic and client-centered practices that prioritize emotional intelligence as a fundamental aspect of the therapeutic relationship. As a result, humanistic psychology has become synonymous with a holistic approach to mental health that respects the individuality of clients.

During the late 1960s and 1970s, humanistic psychology gained traction not only in therapy but also in education, organizational development, and social justice movements. Educational reformers adopted humanistic principles to create more supportive learning environments that fostered emotional intelligence, creativity, and critical thinking. In the workplace, organizations began to recognize the importance of employee well-being and engagement, leading to a more humane approach to management and leadership. This evolution highlighted the relevance of emotional intelligence in various contexts, including conflict resolution and business ethics, as leaders sought to cultivate healthier workplace cultures.

The intersection of humanistic psychology and social justice is particularly noteworthy. As the movement evolved, many humanistic psychologists became advocates for social change, championing causes such as equality, community building, and the enhancement of social values. This advocacy was driven by the belief that addressing systemic issues was essential for fostering individual well-being. Humanistic psychology thus positioned itself as a vital force in various social justice movements, emphasizing the role of emotional intelligence in understanding and addressing societal inequities and conflicts.

Today, the legacy of humanistic psychology continues to influence diverse fields such as parenting, community development, and organizational leadership. Its emphasis on emotional intelligence has become integral to approaches that promote well-being, resilience, and ethical decision-making. As society grapples with complex challenges, the principles of humanistic psychology serve as a guiding framework for redefining success, prioritizing the common good, and fostering a more compassionate and just world. By integrating these principles into everyday practices, individuals and organizations can contribute to a more humane society that values each person's potential and well-being.

CONTRIBUTIONS
to Social Justice

Contributions to social justice have increasingly become a focal point for psychologists, particularly through the lens of humanism. Humanistic psychology emphasizes the inherent value of each individual and the importance of self-actualization, which aligns closely with social justice initiatives. Psychologists engaged in these movements work to dismantle systemic barriers that hinder individuals from realizing their full potential. By applying principles of emotional intelligence, they foster environments where marginalized voices are heard and valued, creating pathways for equitable participation in society.

One significant contribution of humanistic psychology to social justice is the promotion of emotional intelligence as a core competency in leadership development. Leaders who possess high emotional intelligence are better equipped to understand and address the needs of diverse communities. They can navigate complex social issues with empathy and compassion, facilitating inclusive decision-making processes. This approach not only empowers leaders but also cultivates a culture of accountability and transparency, where the well-being of all community members is prioritized over individual gain.

In the context of mental health therapy, humanistic approaches play a vital role in advocating for equitable access to psychological services. Therapists trained in humanistic modalities prioritize the therapeutic relationship, fostering trust and safety for clients from all backgrounds. By emphasizing the importance of empathy and understanding, these practitioners can effectively address the unique challenges faced by marginalized populations. This commitment to social justice within therapy not only promotes individual healing but also contributes to the broader movement for mental health equity.

Conflict resolution is another area where emotional intelligence and humanistic psychology intersect to promote social justice. Understanding and managing emotions are crucial in resolving disputes, particularly in communities facing systemic oppression. By teaching individuals the skills of active listening, empathy, and effective communication, psychologists can help transform conflicts into opportunities for growth and understanding. This process not only resolves immediate issues but also builds social cohesion, fostering resilience in communities striving for justice.

The integration of emotional intelligence into parenting techniques reflects a commitment to nurturing the next generation with strong social values. Parents who practice emotional intelligence are better positioned to instill principles of empathy, cooperation, and respect in their children. This foundation can lead to a more compassionate society where future leaders prioritize social justice. By redefining success through well-being and the common good, humanistic psychology aims to create a world where every individual has the opportunity to thrive, ultimately contributing to a more just and equitable society.

CASE STUDIES OF MOVEMENTS INFLUENCED BY HUMANISTIC PSYCHOLOGY

Humanistic psychology has profoundly influenced various social movements throughout history, fostering a commitment to human dignity, potential, and social justice.

- One notable case is the **civil rights movement of the 1960s**, where leaders like Martin Luther King Jr. exemplified humanistic principles through their advocacy for equality and nonviolent resistance. King's emphasis on love, empathy, and community reflected a humanistic approach that prioritized the inherent worth of every individual. His teachings encouraged followers to cultivate emotional intelligence, enabling them to connect deeply with others and understand the broader implications of their struggle for justice. This movement not only sought to dismantle systemic racism but also aimed to build a more compassionate society, aligning closely with the tenets of humanistic psychology.

In the realm of mental health therapy, the rise of community mental health movements can be seen as a direct application of humanistic values. These movements emerged in response to the inadequacies of institutional care, advocating for more humane and supportive environments for individuals facing mental health challenges. By promoting the idea that every person has the potential for growth and self-actualization, advocates sought to create community-based support systems that empower individuals. This shift towards a more integrated and compassionate approach to mental health care has transformed how society views and addresses mental health, emphasizing the importance of emotional intelligence in both practitioners and patients alike.

- Another compelling case study is **the feminist movement**, which has utilized humanistic psychology to address issues of gender inequality and empowerment. Feminist theorists have integrated concepts of emotional intelligence to highlight the importance of self-awareness, empathy, and relational skills in challenging patriarchal structures. By fostering a sense of community among women and promoting the idea of shared experiences, the movement has encouraged individuals to articulate their needs and aspirations. This focus on emotional intelligence has not only helped in advocating for women's rights but also in redefining success and leadership in a way that values collaboration and mutual support over competition.

- **The environmental movement** also embodies the principles of humanistic psychology, particularly through initiatives that emphasize the interconnectedness of human beings and the natural world. Environmental activists advocate for sustainable practices that respect both individual rights and the collective good, fostering a sense of community responsibility. By integrating emotional intelligence into their messaging, they encourage individuals to develop a deeper emotional connection to nature, promoting stewardship and ethical decision-making. This humanistic approach not only addresses environmental issues but also reinforces the need for wisdom-based decision-making in business ethics, where the well-being of the planet and its inhabitants is prioritized.

The **integration of humanistic psychology within educational reform movements** illustrates the importance of emotional intelligence and social values in shaping future generations. Educators and advocates are increasingly focusing on developing curricula that cultivate emotional intelligence, encouraging students to engage in self-reflection, empathy, and social responsibility. This educational approach aims to foster a culture of well-being, where success is redefined beyond academic achievement to include personal growth and community contributions. By embedding humanistic principles into education, these movements are nurturing a new generation of leaders equipped to navigate complex social challenges with compassion and insight.

EMOTIONAL INTELLIGENCE AND WORKPLACE CULTURE

Understanding Workplace Culture

Understanding workplace culture is essential for fostering an environment where employees can thrive both personally and professionally. Workplace culture encompasses the values, beliefs, behaviors, and practices that shape a company's social and psychological environment. It influences how employees interact with one another, how they perceive their roles within the organization, and ultimately, how effectively they collaborate towards common goals. In the context of emotional intelligence, understanding workplace culture allows leaders to harness the emotional and social aspects of their teams to create a more cohesive and productive workforce.

Emotional intelligence plays a critical role in shaping workplace culture. Leaders who are emotionally intelligent are better equipped to understand and manage their own emotions, as well as those of their team members. This understanding fosters empathy, enhances communication, and reduces conflict, which are vital components of a healthy workplace culture. By modeling emotional intelligence, leaders can create an atmosphere of trust and respect, encouraging employees to express their thoughts and feelings openly. This, in turn, cultivates a culture where feedback is valued and innovation can flourish.

Incorporating humanistic approaches to mental health therapy within workplace culture also contributes to the overall well-being of employees. By prioritizing mental health, organizations can demonstrate that they value their employees as whole individuals rather than just as workers. This approach encourages the development of supportive networks that promote psychological safety, where employees feel secure in sharing their struggles and seeking help when needed. Such a culture not only enhances individual well-being but also improves team dynamics and overall productivity, as employees are less likely to experience burnout or disengagement.

Conflict resolution is another area where a strong workplace culture can make a significant difference. Organizations that prioritize emotional intelligence among their leaders and employees are more likely to navigate conflicts effectively. When team members understand and respect each other's emotional states, they are better positioned to engage in constructive dialogue. This understanding leads to collaborative problem-solving rather than adversarial confrontations, allowing teams to maintain a focus on shared objectives rather than personal grievances. A culture that embraces emotional intelligence thus acts as a foundation for effective conflict resolution, ultimately leading to a more harmonious workplace.

Redefining success through principles of well-being and the common good is essential in cultivating a positive workplace culture. Organizations that align their goals with the values of social responsibility and community building create an environment where employees feel a sense of purpose. When success is measured not only by financial gains but also by the well-being of employees and the impact on the community, it fosters a more engaged and motivated workforce. This shift in perspective encourages individuals to contribute positively to their workplace and society, reinforcing the idea that a thriving workplace culture is intrinsically linked to broader social justice movements.

The Role *of* EI *in* Shaping Positive Cultures

Emotional Intelligence (EI) plays a crucial role in shaping positive cultures across various spheres of society, including workplaces, communities, and interpersonal relationships. In leadership development, EI fosters a climate of empathy and understanding, enabling leaders to connect with their teams on a deeper level. This connection not only enhances communication but also cultivates trust, which is essential for any thriving culture. Leaders who demonstrate high emotional intelligence are better equipped to navigate complex social dynamics, ensuring that their approaches align with the needs and values of their team members.

In the context of mental health therapy, humanistic approaches that integrate EI can lead to more effective therapeutic outcomes. Therapists who possess emotional intelligence are able to create safe environments where clients feel understood and valued. By tuning into clients' emotions and responding with compassion, therapists can facilitate healing and personal growth. This not only improves individual well-being but also contributes to the broader culture of acceptance and support within communities. Such humanistic practices encourage individuals to embrace their emotions, fostering a healthier societal outlook on mental health.

Conflict resolution also benefits significantly from emotional intelligence. EI equips individuals with the skills necessary to approach conflicts with a mindset focused on understanding rather than confrontation. By recognizing and validating the emotions of all parties involved, conflict resolution becomes a collaborative process rather than a battleground. This shift in perspective not only resolves immediate disputes but also strengthens relationships by building a foundation of respect and cooperation. In environments where EI is prioritized, conflicts are viewed as opportunities for growth and learning, thereby enhancing overall community dynamics.

In the sphere of business ethics, wisdom-based decision making rooted in emotional intelligence can redefine traditional notions of success. Leaders who prioritize the common good and well-being of their employees are likely to foster a workplace culture that values ethical considerations alongside profitability. This approach encourages businesses to adopt practices that are socially responsible and sustainable, ultimately contributing to a more equitable society. By integrating EI into their decision-making processes, organizations are not only held accountable for their actions but also inspire a culture of integrity and ethical behavior among their workforce.

Enhancing social values through community building is a fundamental aspect of emotional intelligence. Communities that prioritize EI facilitate connections among individuals, fostering a culture of inclusivity and mutual support. This sense of belonging is essential for collective resilience, enabling communities to address social injustices and advocate for positive change. Moreover, by integrating emotional intelligence into parenting techniques, families can cultivate environments where emotional awareness and social values thrive. This nurturing atmosphere not only benefits children but also extends to the broader community, reinforcing a cycle of empathy and cooperation that is vital for social justice movements.

Strategies *for* Enhancing Workplace EI

Enhancing workplace emotional intelligence (EI) is essential for fostering a collaborative and productive environment. Organizations can adopt several strategies to improve EI among employees, which can lead to better communication, stronger relationships, and increased overall effectiveness. One effective approach is to provide training programs that specifically focus on EI competencies, such as self-awareness, self-regulation, empathy, and social skills. These workshops can utilize role-playing scenarios, group discussions, and self-assessment tools to help participants identify their emotional strengths and areas for improvement. By equipping employees with the necessary skills, organizations can create a more emotionally intelligent workforce.

Another strategy involves integrating EI into the organization's culture. This can be achieved by establishing a set of core values that emphasize emotional awareness and interpersonal connections. Leadership plays a crucial role in modeling these values through their behaviors and decision-making processes. When leaders demonstrate empathy, active listening, and open communication, they set a precedent for employees to follow. This trickle-down effect encourages a culture where emotional intelligence is recognized as a vital component of workplace interactions, ultimately leading to a more cohesive and supportive atmosphere.

Regular feedback mechanisms can also enhance EI within the workplace. Organizations should implement systems for both peer and supervisor feedback that focus on emotional competencies. This can include 360-degree feedback processes, where employees receive insights from multiple sources about their interpersonal skills and emotional responses. By creating an environment where constructive feedback is welcomed and acted upon, employees can gain valuable perspectives on their emotional behaviors and learn how to navigate workplace dynamics more effectively.

Additionally, promoting self-care and mental well-being can significantly influence emotional intelligence in the workplace. Organizations can encourage practices such as mindfulness, stress management workshops, and work-life balance initiatives. When employees feel supported in their mental health, they are more likely to engage positively with their colleagues and manage their emotions effectively. Providing resources for mental health support, such as counseling services or wellness programs, can further reinforce the importance of emotional intelligence as a foundational aspect of workplace culture.

Establishing mentorship programs can facilitate the development of emotional intelligence among employees. Pairing less experienced staff with seasoned mentors can create opportunities for guidance and emotional learning. Mentors can share their insights on managing emotions in challenging situations, fostering resilience, and building positive relationships. This knowledge transfer not only enhances the emotional intelligence of mentees but also strengthens the overall capacity of the organization to navigate conflicts and achieve collaborative success. By implementing these strategies, organizations can cultivate an emotionally intelligent workplace that aligns with humanistic principles and supports both individual and collective well-being.

The silent currents of our inner world, the emotions that course through us like rivers through a hidden landscape, carve the contours of our being, shaping the valleys of our vulnerabilities and the peaks of our triumphs, revealing that true self-knowledge lies not in the mind's grasp, but in the heart's felt experience.

REDEFINING SUCCESS THROUGH WELL BEING AND COMMON GOOD PRINCIPLES

The Shift from Traditional Success Metrics

The shift from traditional success metrics in various sectors reflects a growing recognition of the limitations of conventional measures such as profit margins and productivity rates. Historically, success was often quantified by financial outcomes, market share, or performance evaluations that emphasized individual achievement. However, as society evolves, there is an increasing understanding that these metrics fail to capture the holistic well-being of individuals and communities. This evolution invites leaders, mental health professionals, and organizations to redefine success in ways that resonate with humanistic values, prioritizing emotional intelligence, social connection, and community welfare.

In leadership development, the traditional metrics of success often focused on achieving results at any cost, leading to environments that could foster burnout and disengagement. As organizations embrace emotional intelligence as a core competency, they are beginning to measure success through the lens of employee satisfaction, collaboration, and work-life balance.

Leaders who prioritize emotional intelligence create cultures that value empathy, communication, and authenticity, ultimately leading to sustainable success defined by the collective well-being of their teams and the communities they serve.

Mental health therapy has also seen a paradigm shift, moving away from success metrics that solely emphasize symptom reduction or diagnostic labels. The humanistic approach champions the importance of personal growth, emotional resilience, and the quality of therapeutic relationships. Success is now more frequently evaluated through client empowerment, the development of emotional intelligence, and the fostering of meaningful connections. Practitioners who adopt these principles recognize that true healing and progress encompass more than clinical outcomes; they involve the enhancement of overall life satisfaction and the ability to navigate life's challenges.

In conflict resolution, the traditional metrics often centered around the resolution of disputes or the achievement of specific legal outcomes. However, there is a growing understanding that genuine resolution involves addressing underlying emotional needs and fostering understanding among parties. Emotional intelligence plays a critical role in this process, enabling individuals to engage in dialogue that prioritizes empathy and mutual respect. Success in conflict resolution now includes the cultivation of relationships and the establishment of a shared sense of community, rather than merely the cessation of hostilities.

Business ethics have similarly shifted towards wisdom-based decision-making, where success is defined by the impact of choices on stakeholders and the environment. Organizations are increasingly held accountable for their social and ethical responsibilities, moving beyond profit-driven motives to embrace a broader vision of success that includes sustainability and social equity. Community building through enhanced social values is becoming a key metric for success, as businesses recognize that their long-term viability is intrinsically linked to the health and vitality of the communities in which they operate. This shift reflects a deeper understanding that true success is not merely about individual gain but about contributing positively to the common good.

Incorporating Well-Being Into Success Definitions

Incorporating well-being into definitions of success challenges traditional metrics that prioritize financial gain or status over the holistic health of individuals and communities. Success, often measured by quantifiable achievements, overlooks the essential elements of emotional and psychological well-being. By redefining success to include well-being, we create a more inclusive framework that acknowledges the importance of mental health, emotional intelligence, and community engagement. This redefinition aligns closely with humanistic psychology, which emphasizes the value of the individual and the importance of personal fulfillment as essential aspects of a meaningful life.

The integration of well-being into success definitions necessitates a shift in leadership development paradigms. Leaders who prioritize emotional intelligence foster environments where team members feel valued and understood, contributing to enhanced workplace culture. By recognizing that successful leadership involves nurturing the emotional and mental health of their teams, leaders can promote a culture of well-being that ultimately drives organizational success. This approach not only leads to better employee satisfaction but also creates a ripple effect that can influence the broader community positively.

In the context of mental health therapy, incorporating well-being into success definitions aligns with humanistic approaches that prioritize individual growth and resilience. Therapists who embrace this perspective empower clients to redefine their measures of success, encouraging them to pursue goals that enhance their overall well-being rather than conforming to external societal pressures. This shift can lead to more sustainable mental health outcomes, as individuals learn to value their emotional and psychological health as integral to their overall success in life.

The role of emotional intelligence in conflict resolution is profoundly impacted by a well-being-centered definition of success. In conflicts, understanding and acknowledging the emotional needs of all parties can lead to more compassionate and effective resolutions. When success is viewed through the lens of well-being, mediators and leaders become more adept at fostering environments of empathy and understanding, which are critical in resolving disputes. This approach not only resolves immediate issues but also strengthens relationships and community ties.

In the context of community building, redefining success to include well-being promotes enhanced social values that benefit everyone. Communities that prioritize the common good and individual well-being foster environments of trust and cooperation. By encouraging community members to engage in practices that support collective well-being, such as volunteerism and collaborative problem-solving, we cultivate a culture that celebrates shared success. This redefinition encourages individuals to see their contributions as essential to the health of the larger community, reinforcing the interconnectedness of personal and collective well-being in the pursuit of a just and equitable society.

CASE STUDIES OF RGANIZATIONS REDEFINING SUCCESS

Case studies of organizations redefining success illustrate the transformative potential of humanistic principles in various sectors. **One notable example is Patagonia,** an outdoor apparel company that has woven environmental sustainability and social responsibility into its business model. Patagonia's commitment to quality products is matched by its dedication to ethical practices, such as using recycled materials and ensuring fair labor conditions. The company measures success not solely in financial terms but through its positive impact on the environment and community. By promoting a culture of transparency and accountability, Patagonia demonstrates how aligning business practices with social values can lead to both profitability and a profound sense of purpose.

- Another case study is the **non-profit organization Teach For America (TFA)**, which seeks to address educational inequities across the United States. TFA recruits passionate individuals to teach in under-resourced schools, emphasizing the importance of leadership grounded in empathy and social justice. The organization emphasizes emotional intelligence in its training programs, equipping educators with the skills to build meaningful relationships with students and communities. TFA's success is measured by the long-term impact on educational outcomes and the cultivation of future leaders who are committed to social equity, showcasing the power of humanistic approaches in advancing educational reform.

- In the corporate sector, **the software company Salesforce** has adopted a model of stakeholder capitalism that prioritizes the well-being of employees, customers, and communities alongside financial performance. Salesforce's integrated approach includes initiatives such as equal pay, mental health resources, and community engagement programs. The organization exemplifies how emotional intelligence can enhance workplace culture, fostering an environment where employees feel valued and connected. By redefining success through a lens of collective well-being, Salesforce not only boosts morale but also drives innovation and loyalty, demonstrating that business ethics can align with humanistic values.

- Healthcare organizations are also exploring new definitions of success. **The Cleveland Clinic** has embraced a patient-centered model that prioritizes holistic care and emotional well-being. By integrating mental health services with traditional medical care, the clinic addresses the complexities of patient needs, promoting a culture of compassion and understanding. This humanistic approach not only improves patient outcomes but also enhances staff satisfaction, as healthcare professionals are empowered to connect with patients on a deeper level. Cleveland Clinic's success is indicative of a broader shift in healthcare towards models that recognize the importance of emotional intelligence in fostering healing and trust.

- **Community organizations like the Harlem Children's Zone (HCZ)** illustrate the impact of humanistic principles on social justice initiatives. HCZ employs a comprehensive strategy to support children and families in a 97-block area of Harlem, focusing on education, health, and community engagement. By providing resources and support systems that address the root causes of poverty, HCZ fosters resilience and empowerment among its residents. The organization's success is measured by the holistic improvement of community well-being, showcasing the effectiveness of integrating social values and emotional intelligence into community-building efforts.

These case studies collectively highlight the potential for redefining success in ways that prioritize human dignity, social justice, and collective well-being.

FUTURE DIRECTIONS SUMMARY OF KEY INSIGHTS

The exploration of humanism within the context of social justice movements reveals profound insights into the interconnectedness of psychology and societal progress. One critical understanding is the essential role of emotional intelligence in leadership development. Leaders equipped with high emotional intelligence are better able to navigate complex interpersonal dynamics, fostering inclusive environments that value diverse perspectives. This capability not only enhances team cohesion but also drives collective action toward social justice goals, emphasizing empathy and understanding as foundational leadership qualities.

Humanistic approaches to mental health therapy further underscore the significance of individual experiences and perspectives in healing processes. These therapeutic models prioritize the client's subjective reality, promoting self-actualization and personal growth. By integrating humanistic principles, therapists can empower individuals to confront societal injustices that impact their mental health, facilitating a deeper engagement with both personal and community issues. This alignment of therapy with social values ultimately cultivates a healthier society, as individuals are encouraged to advocate for themselves and others.

In the realm of conflict resolution, emotional intelligence emerges as a pivotal factor in addressing disputes effectively. Understanding one's emotions and those of others allows individuals to approach conflicts with a sense of compassion and insight. This awareness can de-escalate tensions and foster constructive dialogue, paving the way for resolutions that honor the needs of all parties involved. By equipping individuals and leaders with emotional intelligence skills, organizations can create a culture that prioritizes peaceful conflict resolution, enhancing community relationships and promoting social harmony.

The integration of wisdom-based decision-making in business ethics is another key insight. Organizations that prioritize ethical considerations rooted in emotional intelligence can redefine success to encompass not just profit, but also the well-being of individuals and communities. This approach encourages businesses to consider their impact on social justice, cultivating a workplace culture that values integrity, responsibility, and a commitment to the common good. As businesses embrace these principles, they contribute to a broader societal shift towards ethical practices that align with humanistic values.

Finally, the intersection of emotional intelligence and parenting techniques highlights the importance of nurturing future generations with empathy and social awareness. By instilling these values early on, parents can raise children who are not only emotionally intelligent but also socially responsible. This commitment to developing emotional skills in the family unit contributes to community building, as children learn to value cooperation, respect, and social justice from a young age. Ultimately, the insights drawn from humanism in action advocate for a holistic approach to personal and societal well-being, reinforcing the notion that emotional intelligence is fundamental to fostering a just and equitable world.

The Future of Humanism *and* Psychology *in* Social Justice

The future of humanism and psychology in social justice holds significant potential for shaping more equitable societies. As global challenges such as economic inequality, systemic discrimination, and mental health crises become increasingly urgent, the integration of humanistic principles within psychological practice can facilitate transformative change. Humanism emphasizes the inherent dignity and worth of every individual, advocating for a holistic understanding of human experiences. By embracing these values, psychologists can contribute to social justice movements that prioritize emotional intelligence, empathy, and community engagement.

Emotional intelligence plays a crucial role in leadership development, influencing how leaders engage with their teams and communities. Future leaders equipped with strong emotional intelligence can navigate complex social dynamics, fostering inclusive environments that recognize diverse perspectives. By promoting self-awareness and relational skills, humanistic psychology supports leaders in creating cultures of trust and collaboration. This approach not only enhances workplace productivity but also empowers individuals to advocate for social justice, ensuring that marginalized voices are heard and valued.

In the realm of mental health therapy, humanistic approaches can be pivotal in addressing the psychological needs of diverse populations. By prioritizing empathy, active listening, and validation, therapists can create safe spaces for individuals to explore their experiences related to social injustice. As mental health becomes a critical component of overall well-being, integrating humanistic principles can lead to more culturally competent care. Therapists who embrace social justice frameworks can help clients process trauma related to systemic oppression, thereby fostering resilience and agency.

Conflict resolution is another area where the intersection of humanism and psychology can yield positive outcomes. Emotional intelligence equips individuals with the skills to navigate disagreements constructively, fostering understanding and cooperation. In communities affected by conflict, humanistic approaches can facilitate dialogues that prioritize empathy and shared values. By training individuals in emotional intelligence and conflict resolution strategies, social justice advocates can build communities that are not only resilient but also committed to collective well-being.

Ultimately, the future of humanism and psychology in social justice is about redefining success through principles of well-being and the common good. This shift requires a collective commitment to understanding the interconnectedness of human experiences and recognizing that individual well-being is deeply tied to social equity. By fostering emotional intelligence across various domains—leadership, therapy, parenting, and community engagement—society can cultivate an environment where justice, empathy, and human dignity thrive. The integration of humanistic psychology into social justice movements not only enhances individual lives but also paves the way for a more just and compassionate world.

Call *to* Action for Readers

In the pursuit of social justice, the application of humanistic principles can transform not only individual lives but entire communities. As readers, you are urged to reflect on your unique roles within your spheres of influence, whether that be in leadership, therapy, conflict resolution, or community building. Each of you possesses the power to cultivate emotional intelligence, a critical component for fostering understanding and compassion. By integrating these principles into your daily interactions, you can begin to challenge the status quo and promote a culture that values well-being and the common good.

Leadership development is one of the most impactful areas where humanistic psychology can thrive. Leaders who prioritize emotional intelligence are better equipped to inspire and motivate their teams, creating an environment where each individual feels valued and heard. By embracing a humanistic approach, you can lead by example, demonstrating how empathy and active listening can transform workplace culture. Your commitment to these values can ripple outward, influencing not only your organization but also the larger community, encouraging others to adopt similar practices.

In mental health therapy, the humanistic approach emphasizes the importance of empathy, authenticity, and unconditional positive regard. As adults who engage with others, whether as practitioners or supporters, your call to action involves advocating for these principles in therapeutic settings. By promoting emotional intelligence in mental health, you contribute to a more compassionate society where individuals feel safe to express their vulnerabilities and seek help without stigma. This advocacy is vital in breaking down barriers that inhibit access to mental health resources, particularly for marginalized populations.

Conflict resolution is another domain where emotional intelligence plays a crucial role. As you navigate personal and professional relationships, consider how your emotional awareness can facilitate more constructive dialogues. By practicing empathy and understanding differing perspectives, you can help de-escalate tensions and foster reconciliation. This approach not only resolves immediate conflicts but also strengthens community ties and encourages a culture of collaboration and mutual respect. Your actions can serve as a model for others, demonstrating that conflict can be an opportunity for growth rather than division.

Finally, the integration of emotional intelligence into parenting techniques is essential for nurturing the next generation of socially conscious individuals. By modeling emotional awareness and compassion in your parenting, you can instill these values in children, equipping them with the tools they need to navigate a complex world. This investment in their emotional development will ultimately lead to a more just and equitable society. As you engage with these principles in your own lives, remember that your efforts contribute to a larger movement toward social justice, demonstrating that the humanistic approach is not just a theoretical framework but a practical guide for creating lasting change.

Humanity's greatest strength lies not in the cold logic of reason alone, but in the warm embrace of emotional intelligence.
It is in understanding and navigating the currents of feeling that we find our true potential for connection, compassion, and growth.

Emotional intelligence is not merely a personal virtue; it is the cornerstone of a thriving humanity. In a world often fractured by misunderstanding, it is the bridge that spans divides, fosters empathy, and builds a foundation for lasting peace.

EMOTIONS

Grief, a solitary pilgrimage through the barren landscapes of loss, is not the negation of love, but its enduring testament, a sacred space where the echoes of cherished connections continue to resonate, reminding us that the depth of our sorrow is a reflection of the immeasurable value of what we have lost, and of what remains within us.

Joy, the ephemeral spark that ignites the soul, is not merely a fleeting sensation, but a profound communion with the present moment, a recognition of the inherent beauty that permeates the ordinary, a reminder that the universe's symphony of wonder plays within the very chambers of our hearts.

Fear, the shadow that dances at the edges of our awareness, is not a sign of weakness,

but a vital compass, guiding us towards the
untamed territories of our potential, challenging
us to confront the unknown, and revealing that
true courage lies not in its absence,
but in our willingness to walk forward, despite
its chilling presence.

Anger, the fiery crucible of injustice, is not
a destructive force, but a passionate
declaration of our intrinsic worth, a primal cry
for fairness and dignity, a reminder that to
silence our righteous indignation is to deny the
very essence of our humanity and to relinquish
our power to shape a more just world.

Hope, the quiet architect of future
possibilities, is not a naïve illusion, but a
conscious act of creation, a steadfast belief in
the transformative power of the human spirit to
rebuild and reimagine, even from the ashes of
despair, a testament to our innate capacity to
find light in the darkest of nights.

Empathy, the sacred art of inhabiting another's experience, is the bridge that spans the chasm of human isolation, allowing us to perceive the shared humanity that unites us all, revealing the profound interconnectedness of our journeys, and fostering a world where compassion and understanding reign supreme.

Love, the enigmatic and boundless force that permeates the universe, is not merely a sentiment, but the very essence of our being, a profound connection that transcends the limitations of time and space, a reminder that to love and to be loved is to experience the true meaning of existence.